Lifted To The Shoulders
Of A Mountain

Lifted To The Shoulders Of A Mountain

◆

A story of the people who climbed
a mountain before their home became
Little Switzerland, N. C. Their strength
and courage will lift them up.

Pat Turner Mitchell

iUniverse, Inc.
New York Lincoln Shanghai

Lifted To The Shoulders Of A Mountain
A story of the people who climbed a mountain before their home became Little Switzerland, N. C. Their strength and courage will lift them up.

iUniverse books may be ordered through booksellers or by contacting:

iUniverse
2021 Pine Lake Road, Suite 100
Lincoln, NE 68512
www.iuniverse.com
1-800-Authors (1-800-288-4677)

Most characters in this work are historical figures and most events portrayed did take place. However, some of the author's dialogue is fiction. This book is based on family stories of written record and the author's knowledge of the history of the time. Some of the other characters, names, dialogue and events are the product of the author's imagination.

Front cover: Jane and Fons McKinney home place. Oil on canvas signed and dated 1940 by Paul W. Whitener (deceased). Gifted to the author by artist's wife, Mildred McKinney Whitener Coe.

ISBN: 978-0-595-43750-4 (pbk)
ISBN: 978-0-595-88079-9 (ebk)

Printed in the United States of America

This book is in memory of my grandparents, Jane and Fons McKinney, my parents, Edith and David Turner, our families, and my dear friend Nancy Pearson.

It is dedicated to my husband Jack Mitchell, my brother Jim Turner, my sister Janice Cline, and all our extended families.

Contents

Book II

Book III

Prologue

1944

I have many memories of my grandparents, Jane and Fons McKinney, but my thoughts today go back to a warm summer day when I was about eight years old. I remember Grandmother (Granny) Jane sitting on her back porch in Little Switzerland. I see her there, face lined and soft, leaning close to me. Her coronet of plaited, white hair has wisps coming loose and I tuck a strand behind her ear. Her dress is soft, faded cotton and she wears thick stockings and leather shoes laced to fit her foot. She bends her long torso closer to me and I smell a faint odor of snuff. Laughing, she pats my cheek. Her long fingers pick up another pod of the last green peas of the season. She pops it open and strips the peas, as she shows me how it's done.

I hear water spilling out of the pipe fed from my grandfather's (Papa Fons) spring. It splashes on a bed of rock before spilling down the hill to the creek. A plank of wood allows you to cross this water from the garden. Its specific purpose now is to wash vegetables fresh from the garden with icy cold spring water. I see him there washing the green onions and lettuce, leaving them under the running water. Then he walks to the porch carrying a bucket.

He wears a hat to shade his face. His shirt is gray, soft from many washings. He reaches into the bucket and pulls out a handful of red raspberries. I cup my hands under his and feel his crooked little finger. He spills the berries into my hands then removes his hat. He combs his grizzled hair with his fingers and sits on the steps. I move beside him and offer him a raspberry. His blue eyes are grave as he accepts it. His face tempts me to lean close and kiss his cheek.

I didn't know then that my time with them would be short. Papa died when I was seventeen, Granny, when I was twenty. I hold them, and their time, and place, close in my heart. I remember it all so vividly. I can close my eyes and walk in each room of their house.

The cozy kitchen had a wood fired cook stove. On the wall beside it was a large ceramic sink, where a stream of icy water came from the spigot. On the opposite wall from the stove was a white cabinet with stored flour and cornmeal. Granny made her cornbread and drop biscuits on the cabinet counter. A door opened beside it with stairs leading down to the side yard. I remember a small table with two chairs sitting in front of a window between these two walls. Here I had those "drop biscuits" with wild strawberry jam and Papa's best "country sausage" for breakfast. This room was also the place where washtubs were put before the cook stove to be filled with warm water for baths.

The dining room had a long dining table with benches, Jane's pie safe, and a hall tree with a mirror beside the outside door. (The pie safe had originally belonged to Jane's first husband and was brought from their house.) The long dark hall to the living room seemed endless and scary when I was eight. Two bedrooms opened off this hall that took me to the living room.

I remember it had a big open fireplace which helped warm the large bedroom that opened off that room. I've been told that while rocking "high" in my child size rocker, I pitched into the blazing fire. I was too young to remember, but I was burned and lost some hair before Papa Fons rescued me. He dug potatoes from under the snow and shaved the pulp to apply to my burns. In my earliest memory of this room, I'm standing on tiptoe to look over the sill of the window beside the fireplace. It is Christmas night. My dad, David Turner, Papa Fons, and others, walked straight up in front of this house, past what is now Chestnut Grove Church Road, and on to the "Scenic Highway" (now known as The Blue Ridge Parkway). They lit fireworks, celebrating this special night. My three-year-old mind will never forget the sight.

Later, I remember a large potbellied stove that had a kettle of simmering water to give moisture to the air. There was a lovely oil painting of Jane hanging in this room, painted by her son-in-law, Paul W. Whitener. My brother, Jim, has this painting now. Hanging on another wall was a print of a Dutch family sitting around a table looking at a caged bird. I've often wondered where this picture came from.

Out the door, I go down the road to the barn, where Papa tried to teach me to milk his cow, past the corn crib, up the road to Effie's house (Granny's daughter from a previous marriage,) and back. I come across the back yard to the little house where Granny's mother, Nancy, lived for a time. First it was a smokehouse, and later an artist's studio. She took her meals with the McKinney family before she moved into the house. I walk down to the apple house, back up past the gooseberry bushes, across the creek to the garden, and then to the apple orchard, where I pick early apples. Then I go down to Lawrence's house, Papa's son from a previous marriage.

I remember so much of my time with them, but I have a need to tell their story and I don't know them. I only know my grandparents.

Jane and Fons McKinney were born in the aftermath of this country's Civil War and lived through two world wars. During this time, Jane, and women like her, won the right to vote. As I learn the details of their lives before my time, I will write their history as a story. This approach will require dialogue that seems natural to these events.

Children of Mary Jane Buchanan Snipes McKinney and James Alphonzo McKinney: Effa (Effie) Louisa Snipes married Lafayette (Fate) McKinney (both deceased)—Children are Ruby McKinney Buchanan, Earl McKinney, Lewis McKinney (deceased), and Betty McKinney Mace.

Lawrence McKinney married Grace Collis (both deceased)—Children are Guy McKinney (deceased), Robert McKinney, Nina McKinney Bowman, Jerry McKinney, Mildred McKinney Guthrie (deceased), Ralph McKinney, Evelyn McKinney Stockton, and Nancy McKinney Hicks.

Ida Jones McKinney married Gaylord Burleson (both deceased)—Children are Rodney Burleson and Ila Gail Burleson McFalls.

Thelma Anne McKinney married Lawrence Sparks, and second, Carroll Abee (all deceased).

Mildred (Mickey) Missouri McKinney married Paul W. Whitener (deceased), and second, Richard (Dick) Coe (deceased).

Edith Rae McKinney married David Ellis Turner (both deceased)—Children are Patricia Anne Turner Mitchell, James Ellis Turner, and Janice Jane Turner Cline.

Buchanan Home, 2006. Photograph taken by Judy Carson.

Buchanan Home, ca 1920. From left, Nancy Deweese Buchanan and
Mary Deweese Biddix, sisters taking care of the flowers.

Introduction

Little Switzerland, North Carolina, 2006

Across the Blue Ridge Parkway from The Switzerland Inn, and to the left of Grassy Creek Falls Road, sits an old hand-cut board house built in the last decade of the nineteenth century. The roof over the porch is leaning to the ground now and one of its two rock chimneys is completely gone. Some of the red tin roof, which replaced the homemade wood split-shingles, has been ripped off, probably by the wind. The house is almost hidden in the rolling terrain.

My grandmother, Jane Buchanan (Snipes, McKinney), her parents, William and Nancy Deweese Buchanan, and two of her siblings, moved to this house when it was built.

This book will be about how my grandparents, Jane Buchanan Snipes and James Alphonzo (Fons) McKinney, came together. Their marriage brings together two families whose histories were connected from the late 1700's. It tells the story of how these people lived before and during the Civil War and in the late nineteenth and early twentieth centuries. They and their families were brought abruptly into the lives of "city folk" from Charlotte, N.C. in 1909. It is how they became part of the community that became Little Switzerland, N. C.

I learned that my grandparents first lived in a two-story log house, down below her parent's home, from my mother's sister, Mildred Missouri (Mickey) Whitener Coe. Mildred is the only surviving child of Jane and Fons. The land transactions I list later in this Introduction, and the information I received from my cousin, Earl McKinney, gives credibility that the house is where my grandfather, Fons, grew up.

William A. Buchanan, husband of Nancy Deweese Buchanan, with the help of their sons and his brothers, built their house. Nancy was once a well-known figure to people of this area and is still to our family. The Buchanan Cemetery at the Switzerland Inn has a monument to her as well as the family graves. William (Bill) Buchanan, who died in 1903, has been a person whose role in our family history has almost been forgotten. The records I have found puts him back in the story.

I have a copy of the History of Turkey Cove Baptist Church, 1885–1969, written by Mrs. Mamie Hollifield, historian. This church is located in McDowell County, down the mountain a bit from Little Switzerland, on what is now 226A. This was the best road from Marion to Little Switzerland, in the 1930's. The history has William, Nancy, and Alford (Bud) Buchanan, their first son, as charter members when it was organized in 1885. Jane was about 9 years old at this time. The meeting was held in a one-room schoolhouse after a revival there. William and Bud were both teachers and could have been teaching in this school at that time. We have William's teaching certificates qualifying him to teach, beginning in 1860 through 1897. They were listed in the newly organized church as follows: Bud was Sunday School Superintendent and singing leader in 1887; W. A. Buchanan was Sunday School Superintendent in 1889. William and Nancy moved to Grassy Creek after this time.

I believe Bill Buchanan taught in a little school down below the Switzerland Store after they moved to Grassy Creek. When I was visiting my grandparents many years ago there was only a small post office and store made of native (blue granite) rock. You can still see the original building in the midst of the additions made later. My mother told me about the back room of the store. Back then it was used by a barber, who also practiced dentistry when a tooth needed extracting. Much was made of what ended up on the floor in that back room. I remember walking daily to this post office for mail during my summer visits.

The registered deeds show the Buchanan land owned by William A., Daniel L. (Dock), and Elizabeth Hollifield Buchanan (son and mother to William A.) in Grassy Creek Township. It was likely inherited from Joseph W. Buchanan through William's father, Joseph H. Buchanan. This information was included in an option to buy land from Emily Hollifield Buchanan (daughter-in-law of Nancy) and Daniel L. (Dock) Buchanan by Reid Queen for the Switzerland Company, July 13, 1909.

William A. Buchanan died in 1903, seven years before my grandparents were married. My mother, Edith McKinney Turner, and her sisters grew up with Nancy sometimes living in their house, after she "gave up housekeeping." Before I started this book I knew little about Bill Buchanan other than he had taught school and fought and was wounded in the Civil War. I didn't know if he fought for the North or the South, although my relatives expressed amazement that he would have fought for the Union. Yancey, McDowell, and what was to become Mitchell, were counties that had men who stole away into the dark of night, going north to fight for the Union Army. Those who lived through the war sometimes had to continue the fight at home after the war ended. Today those men who fought for the North and the South may be found buried side by side in our cemeteries.

By reading books of family histories compiled by Lloyd Bailey, I found a record of the births and deaths of Nancy and William A. Buchanan's children taken from their family Bible. This helped enormously in writing about the events we know about this family. At a later time my sister and I were able to hold this Bible in our hands and see the notations that they made about these births and deaths. Here I also learned of William's mother and father, Joseph H. and Elizabeth Hollifield Buchanan.

I have also found William A. Buchanan's 'Last Will and Testament' when it was probated in Superior Court. I am beginning to find records of how his land was disbursed, after his death, but before Nancy died. This information clarifies our family history.

Adjoining the Buchanan property, many acres of land were owned by George Rufus Dale, father to Susan E. Dale, my grandfather's mother. I believe that Susan E. Dale, who was married to Robert Pendley McKinney, inherited land across Grassy Creek down below Nancy and William Buchanan's house. I don't know if they built the two-story log home they lived in there or if, maybe, Susan and her siblings had lived there with her parents before she inherited this property. I have copies of the following registered deeds:

Mitchell County, Book 59, page 546, January 27, 1883, showed George Rufus Dale as deceased and George R. Dale, minor, receiving 55 acres on Grassy Creek, with signatures of James A. Dale, Susan E. (Dale) McKinney, and Jane (Dale) McKinney, Rachel (Dale) McBee (widow), and spouses of Susan and Jane, Robert P. and Tom McKinney.

Mitchell County, Book 45, page 145, February 10, 1899, showing G.R. Dale and his wife E. F. Dale selling 108 acres to R. P. McKinney and wife S. E. McKinney for $500. From what I can discern this is the property where Robert built his gristmill.

Mitchell County, Book 57, page 536, February 15, 1899 (five days later), R. P. McKinney, and wife S. E. McKinney sold 80 acres adjoining W. A. Buchanan, etc. to G. R. Dale for $300.

My grandfather, Fons McKinney, was born to Robert P. and Susan Dale McKinney. Robert was born to Charles McKinney, Jr. and Elizabeth Washburn. Charles McKinney, Jr. was born to Charles McKinney and Nancy Triplett. *(See References at the back of this book for an alphabetical list of characters from this book. There are also land deeds and letters of interest to the community of Little Switzerland that belonged to my grandfather, James Alphonzo (Fons) McKinney.)*

The family photographs and paintings are in this book by the expertise and good graces of Judy Carson. She and my sister, Janice, have been enthusiastic readers of my many drafts and Judy is responsible for the layout of the graphics in this book. Thank you, Judy. There's an interesting story about how the life-size oil painting of Jane and Fons McKinney's daughters, painted by Frank Stanley Herring, was found. Look for it in the Epilogue. This painting is mentioned in *The Story of Little Switzerland.*

I would like to thank Elizabeth M. Rouse McClure, Sarah Dashiel Rouse Sheehan, and Parke Shepherd Rouse, Jr. for giving me permission to use portions of their father's book, *The Great Wagon Road* by Parke Rouse. I would also like to thank Jim Duls, nephew of Louisa DeSaussure Duls, for his permission to use portions of her book, *The Story of Little Switzerland.*

I thank my wonderful family for sharing their memories that have opened doors to this story. Special thanks go to my aunt, Mildred (Mickey) McKinney Whitener Coe, cousins Ruby McKinney Buchanan, Betty McKinney Mace, Earl McKinney (children of Effie Snipes McKinney), Verdie Mae Smith Cox (granddaughter of Melissa Buchanan Schism), and Tom Buchanan (grandson of John Henry Buchanan). In telling this story I have added dialogue that seems logical in these events. I have noted all information that is attributed to others. Any errors you may find in this book are solely my own.

These are tintypes in Nancy Buchanan's possession at her death. Top left: William A. Buchanan and Nancy Deweese Buchanan on their wedding day, ca 1860.

Nancy's mother, Rachel McKinney Deweese Lowery, age 63. The young man is her youngest child by Alexander Lowery, John F. Lowery, about age 17. He was born to them in 1860. (Photo, ca 1877)

Rachel's second husband, Alexander Lowery, about age 30, just before he left for the Civil War. He joined the 35th NC that was formed on September 11, 1861. He died in Richmond VA in 1861. (Photo ca 1861)

Tintype identification and information is by John McKinney, Marion, NC

Effa Louisa (Effie) Snipes and Jane
Buchanan Snipes, ca 1908.

Zebulan Vance Snipes, Effie's father, ca
1883–1888 (about ten or fifteen years
before he married Jane Buchanan.)

Zebulan Vance Snipes (holding infant Effie) and Jane Buchanan Snipes,
April or May 1899. (Photograph is from a tintype.)

Lawrence McKinney, son of Fons and Hattie Waycaster McKinney,
Jane B. Snipes McKinney, and Ida Jones McKinney held
by J. Fons McKinney, 1911.

Decoration Day at Buchanan Cemetery, ca 1920. Jane B. Snipes
McKinney in hat.

Susan Dale and Robert P. McKinney, ca 1920. Photograph given to author by Hilda and Frank Hollifield.

Postcard of Little Switzerland Grist Mill. It looks like the mill of Robert McKinney.

John Henry Buchanan, (brother of Jane B. Snipes McKinney and Melissa
B. Schism) and wife, Emma Jane Elliott Buchanan.

Front left, Mary Deweese Biddix and her sister Nancy Deweese Buchanan.
Back left, Melissa B. Schism and her sister, Jane B. Snipes McKinney
at the Buchanan home beside Grassy Creek Road.

Characters in "Lifted To The Shoulders Of A Mountain"

(Mary) Jane Buchanan—My grandmother, second daughter of Nancy Deweese and William A. Buchanan. She married Zebulon Vance Snipes on February 27, 1898 and second, married J. Fons McKinney on June 17, 1910. She was born August 21, 1876 and died August 28, 1956.

Nancy Deweese Buchanan—My great-grandmother, daughter of Rachel McKinney and Louis Deweese. She married William A. Buchanan on November 11, 1860. She was born February 2, 1842 in Missouri and died August 26, 1935 in Little Switzerland, N. C.

Rachel Jane McKinney Deweese Lowery—My great-great grandmother, first daughter of Charles McKinney and Elizabeth Lowery. She had one brother from this union, Alexander McKinney, who was killed when a log rolled over him when he was about 28 years old. Rachel married Louis Deweese, who died near St. Louis, Missouri, in 1847. Rachel returned with her family, daughters Nancy, Jane and Mary Elizabeth, to N. C. She married Alexander Lowery in 1850. At her father's death in 1852, he left her 100 acres of land at Pepper's Creek. (N. C. Records) She was born ca 1814 and died in 1904.

William A. Buchanan—My great-grandfather, son of Joseph H. Buchanan and Elizabeth Hollifield Buchanan (my great-great grandparents.) Married Nancy Deweese in November of 1860 and leaves on July 4, 1861 to go to war. He taught school beginning in 1860, fought in the Civil War, then returned to teaching through 1897. He was born April 26, 1839 and died April 26, 1903.

John Robert (Bob) Buchanan—He is the son of Joseph H. Buchanan and Elizabeth Hollifield Buchanan. Brother to William A., Alford A., and George Buchanan. Married Rebecca (Becky) Snipes, sister to Zebulon Vance

Snipes. Robert and Rebecca Buchanan are Carrie Washburn's grandparents.

Zebulon Vance Snipes—Married Jane Buchanan February 27, 1898. Child: Effa (Effie) Louisa. He was born April 28, 1856 and died May 31, 1908.

Martha Melissa Buchanan—She is the first child of Nancy and William (Bill) Buchanan. She was born September 8, 1861 and died June 10, 1939. Married Molt Schism September 12, 1886.

Alford A. (Bud) Buchanan—First son of Nancy and Bill Buchanan, born May 29, 1864, conceived while Bill was home during the war. Named for Bill's brother, Alford A. Buchanan, who was killed in the Civil War at The North Anna River in May of 1864. Bud married Sally Ann Elliott, April 9, 1891. He died April 3, 1898, at age 34, of consumption. Sallie Ann died April 18, 1903.

John Henry Buchanan—Second son of Bill and Nancy, born March 21, 1866 and died in 1939. Married Emma Jane Elliott September 8, 1891, sister of Sallie Ann.

William P. Buchanan—Third son, born June 3, 1868 and died March 5, 1874 of diphtheria.

James D. Buchanan—Fourth son, born December 28, 1870 and died March 8, 1874 of diphtheria.

Daniel L. (Dock) Buchanan—Fifth son, was born April 23, 1873 and died September 16, 1910 at age 37. He married Dovie McBee December 3, 1893.

Joseph Neal Buchanan—Sixth son, born April 23, 1878. He married Emily A. Hollifield February 1, 1902. He died December 16, 1908, age 30, falling from a railroad trestle at Bostic Junction, N. C.

Lula E. Buchanan—Third daughter, born July 10, 1881, died at age 21 on February 15, 1903. She had meningitis (or something similar) when she was two or three years old. She was unable to walk or feed herself after surviving the illness.

James Alphonzo (Fons) McKinney—My grandfather, first son of Robert and Susan Dale McKinney. Born August 19, 1881. He married Hattie Waycaster September 25, 1900, who died in 1904. They had two sons, Lawrence and Wayne. Married Hester Stafford, date unknown. They were divorced, date unknown. He married (Mary) Jane Buchanan Snipes, June 17, 1910. Children: Ida Jones, Thelma Anne, Mildred Missouri and Edith Rae. He died April 26, 1953.

Robert P. McKinney—My great-grandfather, the youngest son of Charles McKinney, Jr. and Elizabeth Washburn McKinney. Born ca 1857 and died 1925. Owned and operated a gristmill. Married Susan Dale.

Susan Dale—My great-grandmother, daughter of George Dale and Rachel Mace Dale, my great-great grandparents. Born 1860 and died 1935.

Charles McKinney, Jr.—My great-great grandfather (half-brother of Rachel McKinney), born ca 1817 and died February 1, 1862. His parents were Charles McKinney and Nancy Triplett, my great-great-great grandparents. He married Elizabeth Washburn, born June 11, 1823 and died January 10, sometime in the 1880's.

Charles McKinney—My great-great-great grandfather, born ca 1780 and died ca 1852. Married Elizabeth Lowery March 7, 1813 (N. C. Records), my great-great-great grandmother. There were two children, Rachel and Alexander. McKinney Gap on the Blue Ridge Parkway is named for Charles and is said to be close by where his families lived. According to stories and census records he had four families (or more) located in the same area. (I am listing only my family connections in this record.)

Book I

1

Jane Buchanan, February 1898, in Grassy Creek, Mitchell County N.C.

I don't know why I need to tell my grandmother's story, but I do. She and my grand-father influenced my life. My memories of them are of emotion: love, beauty of spirit, and a feeling of security. I am here, close by their place because it feels like home to me. When I leave here and first glimpse the mountains on my return, my body relaxes. I am coming home. I have moments when I want them to be here, in their home place. My widowed mother, in her last years, would ask to go "home" sometimes, when visit-ing here with us. Jane and Fons are home, lifted to the shoulders of a mountain.

Jane lived in a time and culture that is different from our time. Her mother arranged a marriage for her. Instead of allowing her to stay in a safe place, where she was needed, Nancy pushed her out to sink or swim. Her father may have been fright-ened for her, but both parents sent her out. Nancy had "chosen" a good man that they both believed would make a good husband for Jane. Her experiences begin here; part of what made her the woman who became my grandmother.

The house is quiet as Jane begins to remove her clothes. The candle sitting on the small table gives enough light to see her empty bed with the covers turned back. Pulling her nightgown over her head, she sits on the bed, then turns and looks around the little attic room.

This was not her usual sleeping place, but one giving her privacy before leav-ing home. It didn't give her comfort. It probably wasn't meant for that purpose. She knew. A separation from her loved ones was the first push to the edge of the nest. The next step was hers. Could she jump and just fly away?

Jane is tall and regal with long limbs and strong hands. She has a clear, dewy complexion. Her dark brown eyes have an innocence and gentleness that is in keeping with her sheltered life. Her beautiful roan hair compliments her coloring. She begins removing the pins and it spills down her back.

Tomorrow she is to be married, an arrangement by her mother, Nancy Buchanan. Shivering in the cooling room, she can't seem to stop the tears that begin to slide down her cheeks. She doesn't know him. Her mind asks if she might come to love him. What if she never could?

◆

Her mother had prepared refreshments for family and neighbors who came for the wedding: homemade cider, cookies, and cake.

Bill Buchanan's mother, Elizabeth, and her sister Sarah Hollifield, live close by and were special guests. Elizabeth Hollifield Buchanan was in her 86th year and had been a widow for some years. Bill and her other sons made sure they were well cared for.

Most of Jane's siblings were here to celebrate her wedding day. Her brother, John Henry, said this day reminded him of his wedding some seven years before and the celebration with their friends. Nancy had prepared their attic room for him and Emma Jane (Elliott) until they could build their own home. They had retired to their room already when they heard loud banging and voices raised in song. Emma Jane laughed as John mimed their friends and family beating pots, clanging bells, and such. Jane was thankful she and her new husband would be far away on their wedding night.

Her elder sister, Melissa, and her husband, Molt Schism, had stayed at home. She was expecting a baby about April and they needed to stay close by home to tend their younger children.

Jane's oldest brother Bud (Alford, named for his dad's brother) was wasting away with consumption. Their children were here, reminding Jane of how much she still loved her sweet brother. Bud, who her father had trained to be a teacher, had been on crutches as long as Jane could remember, due to a childhood illness. He was like their father in his courage and determination, but these attributes couldn't stand up against this illness.

Dock (Daniel) and Dovie were still like newly weds, even after five years. Dock was the teaser, but his brown eyes always conveyed deep affection when he looked Jane's way. She worried about his easy-going ways, always hoping he would stand up to adversity. His look today conveyed sadness for Jane's unhappy, but stoic, determination to do her mother's bidding.

Joe, the youngest son, and Lula, would still be at home when Jane left. Lula had become ill with a high fever when she was two or three years old. Her body began to convulse, jerking and curving in on itself. For days she was unable to take nourishment, but Nancy and Bill worked to cool her little body while squeezing moisture into her mouth. She lived but was no longer able to lift her head or move her limbs. She could only take soft foods, so Nancy chewed the meat and vegetables for her daughter.

Five years apart, Jane and Lula loved and depended on the other's presence in their lives. Jane had slept close by her sister to help tend her during the night. It was a usual routine to rise in the night to change her clothes, after bathing away the smell of her body's waste.

Nancy with Jane's help tended her like a baby. She carried her from her bed to a chair outside when the weather was good. Lula loved to look at the flowers Nancy planted close to the house, and the beans she had trailing up the porch. She listened and seemed to know each bird call. Jane worried about leaving Lula and her mother, though she knew Joe and her dad would help. They didn't have much time after seeing to the farm, and her father was still teaching school, although he would retire soon. Mostly, she would miss Lula's presence in her own life.

Joe reminded Jane of her father. They both had beautiful voices and liked to sing the old hymns at Meeting. Jane has a good alto voice and would join in as they sang sitting around the fire in the evening.

Jane loved her family and hated leaving them. Her heart hurt that Nancy had insisted on this marriage. She could have wanted to keep her at home. There was much to do. She looked at her mother's strength in standing up to adversity, and her father's courage. What events would shape her character? Would she be strong or buckle to her knees?

◆

Her future husband had brought an extra horse up the mountain to get her. Jane and Zebulon Vance Snipes, bachelor, and forty years old to her twenty-one, were to marry on this day, February 27, 1898.

With these thoughts swirling in her head Jane and Vance exchange vows while family and friends look on. They accept the company's smiles and jokes about their coming intimacy. Looking out at the quiet land, while standing on the porch of her parent's house, they prepare to leave.

The mountains look gray with the trees bare. The sun, outlining each limb with an artist's charcoal, gives spring-like warmth to the day. The house sits with a mountain at its back and to its right looks out at Buchanan's Ridge. Jane's grandmother, Elizabeth Hollifield Buchanan, and her sister, Sarah Hollifield, live in the small house close by, snug beneath this protected place. Small knolls roll away in front of the houses until mountains rise, as though standing guard to stop the world from coming here. Orchards stretch to the rolling fields, the trees lifting skeleton like arms towards the sky, and ending at Susie and Robert McKinney's place, a two-story log house across from a roiling creek. Looking west, dark clouds hover close to earth, making rain likely by evening.

The barn and fenced area is to the left of the two houses where several horses graze. Beyond is the enclosure for the young pigs with enough distance between to keep the smell away. They will roam free when a little larger, until they are put up to be fed corn for three or four weeks before slaughter. The cows have been turned out to browse in this welcome sunshine. A working dog is quiet by the steps, while the sheep are scattered across the hill, below the wooded area to the right of the house.

Grassy Creek Falls Road, a wagon road which was passable when dry, runs along side these properties, going on past Grassy Creek Falls to Spruce Pine. The falls must have been a popular place where Susan and Robert McKinney's children would have taken advantage. (My mother, Edith, and her sisters, used Grassy Creek Falls as a place to play and cool off in the summer when they were young.)

William and Nancy Buchanan had raised their family in McDowell County around Turkey's Cove. This house in Grassy Creek is newly built. A door opens from the porch leading to finished stairs going to the attic. The door to the living area opens to a room with a large fireplace in the back of the room. To the left is the kitchen where a smaller fireplace is used for cooking. There is a bedroom to the right of the living area. The living area and kitchen are paneled, possibly in walnut or cherry.

These farms, and the people who live here in 1898, supply the food, clothes, and implements of living that they need. The bed ticks and pillows are filled with goose feathers plucked and gathered, sometimes from the screeching birds. Bed covers are woven from thread made from flax grown here, and wool gathered from the sheep. Our family has a wool, herringbone design coverlet, black, and rust colored, woven by Nancy. The cloth for garments may have been woven from the same thread, but dyed from plants that give their gold, rust, or black hues. The furniture is shaped and carved by Bill Buchanan, Nancy's husband, as was the lumber and the paneling of their house.

Jane and Vance turn and watch the minister approach them, holding a book under his arm. He shakes the groom's hand, takes and releases Jane's hand, then walks down the steps. Opening the gate to the fence surrounding the house, he walks to a hobbled horse. He swings into the saddle and rides past, waving, as he heads toward the road. Nancy and Bill come to the porch and Nancy puts her arms around her daughter. Bill and Vance walk to the barn.

◆

"You have a good farm here." Vance Snipes speaks to his new father-in-law, while leading his horse toward the gate.

Bill Buchanan looked around. "With Nancy and our children, we have done well. All this land once belonged to my grandfather, J. W. Buchanan. Some now belongs to Nancy and me, and some to Mother, who lives in the house close by. I've bought properties for my sons, John and Bud, and my daughter, Melissa. Dock has his own place, too. Melissa and Dock live close by and John Henry and Bud live down the mountain a bit."

"That mountain top you see to the right of the house? That's called Buchanan's Ridge. There's a cemetery there."

He looks at the younger man. "We'll miss Jane, Mr. Snipes. With her brothers, sisters, and our families close, she's had her share of attention." Pausing, he continued. "I know my brother, Bob, and Becky, your sister, look forward to having her close, but I worry. You'll take care of her?"

The younger man cleared his throat. "I will take care of her, sir."

Bill Buchanan thought how Jane needed the love and closeness of her family around her. He wondered if she was strong enough to take life's offerings. She loved going to Peppers Creek, where her maternal grandmother, Rachel McKinney Deweese Lowery, and other McKinney and Lowery kin, surrounded her. Would Vance Snipes' family give her this needed companionship?

His brother, Bob, had married Rebecca Snipes, Vance's sister. Bill and Nancy had visited them many times and had taken Jane with them. The Buchanan's knew Vance's family. The problem was distance from them since they were now in Grassy Creek.

Jane met her father outside the gate. He hugged her tightly then helped her to mount her horse. She and her new husband were ready to begin their journey. They rode off, she sidesaddle, not looking back.

2

Beginnings

Vance smiled, seeing the glaze of tears in her eyes. "Jane, you'll like our farm. I've made the house nice for you, though you may want to change a few things."

She looked at him as he moved his mount close by hers. His dark hair and eyes showed stark against his thin, pale face. He is kind and maybe that helps, she thought, as her mind turned to the coming night. As Granny Rachel says, I'm a woman grown and getting married up will show my mettle. Squaring her shoulders, she eased her grip on the reins.

As if reading her mind, he spoke. "We'll stop at a pretty spot in a few hours, where we can rest and walk about. I reckon it as a place I thought you would like." Their horses began to pick their way down the slope as Vance moved out in front.

He looked back and saw how erect she sat her horse. Her head was slightly bent showing her strong neck and shoulders. She had removed her hat and her brown hair glinted red in the sun. She's strong, he thought, tall and well formed. Thinking of the last months, he pondered the fact that he tired too easily now. If my strength holds out, we'll be all right.

Her strong hands tightened on the reins as the slope became steep. "Mr. Snipes," she called. "You noticed my daddy. He hasn't been well for a long time. Can we visit, come back up the mountain some?"

"Jane, call me Vance, please. We're husband and wife now." Hoping to ease her, he turned and smiled. "There're many jobs to do on the farm. You know all that, but we should be able to come back up before long. Don't fret, Jane. It'll be all right."

Jane tried to smile and nodded. Her thoughts turned to her daddy. Although he was still teaching school, going to renew his teaching certificate every other year, as long as she could remember his health had been frail. Jane knew he had been shot in the war over ten years before she was born. Her heart ached at leaving him.

◆

Bill Buchanan's body was weak but his spirit was strong. Although his carriage was beginning to stoop a little, his tall frame was still imposing, and, oh, his handsome face. A strong face, with dark eyes framed by full brows, and dark hair heavily laced with gray, it showed a countenance of calm acceptance. Knowing his courage of overcoming his physical complaints helped Jane accept her present situation.

"Now Jane," he had said. "Mr. Snipes seems a good man. He is well fixed and that is what your mother wants for you." Jane remembers his eyes as he looked past her to his wife. Then noticing Jane's wan expression, he had put his arms around her. "We've done well all these years, so don't you fret about us. We'll be all right, Nancy and me." Smiling, he had caught her hand in his. "You know I'm sending some of my books with you."

Jane's love for books is a constant joy to him, a love that father and daughter share. She thought of the time he saw her at the spinning wheel, with her book propped on it so she could read while she worked. Her mother probably wasn't pleased since the yarn coming off would show her lack of attention.

Well educated, the Buchanan's had come to Burke County from Rutherford County with 14 other couples in 1808. (Yancey and McDowell Counties would be formed from this part of Burke County.) There is historical information that they moved down from Maryland around 1804, along with the Greenlee's, and others of the more prosperous of their neighbors. The story goes that they stopped here because of a snowstorm, but stayed because of the beauty of the area.

When Bill and Nancy Deweese met, he was a teacher. Teaching was a matter of traveling on horseback to a cabin where children needed instruction in reading, 'riting, and 'rithmatic. Jane could imagine him astride his beautiful horse, face glowing with health. Her mother would have had no choice but to fall in love with him.

Later the children met in one-room schools provided by interested parents. Reading was done mostly in the family bible and Bill's personal library. After the war he began teaching again in the crude one-room schools that had remained empty while he was gone. Despondent as well as in poor health, he thought it was all he could do. Soon his love of teaching helped heal his sore heart. According to history, some six years after the end of the war, due to government waste, extrav-

agance, and deliberate fraud in North Carolina, the school system lost income
and schools. In western North Carolina schools were closed for two years.

Always a clever man, Bill began buying and selling land and properties. He kept
good acreage for himself, and sold tracts to his two oldest sons, and daughter, Melissa, at a good price. Melissa and Molt Schism sold their land in McDowell County
at a profit and bought more land close by Chestnut Grove. Bud and John Henry
built homes on their land. Each was to pay $.50 an acre to Nancy. Joe was the
youngest and he would stay in the home place to take care of Nancy and Lula until
their deaths. Bill arranged this since he felt he would not live to old age, because of
his fragile health. Dock and Jane would receive land in his Will.

◆

Jane glances at her husband who is beginning to slow his pace. They are coming into a little valley, with a small grouping of trees just ahead. He turns, his eyes
going from her face to her erect body sitting her horse. "Are you tired, Jane? Just
ahead is our rest spot. There's a spring just there in the trees."

It was a good place to stop. Her husband allowed the horses to graze the winter grass and had brought water to them in his hat. Jane found a sheltered place
close by the spring to eat their picnic. She laid out fried chicken, apples, and biscuits. Everything was serene and peaceful except her thoughts. She wondered if
she could eat. It seemed like a large lump blocked her throat. Looking around
her, she shivered. She was alone with a stranger.

Her mind wandered back to the time she first saw Vance. She had gone along
with her mother and dad when they traveled to Buck's Creek to visit her Uncle
Robert (Bob) Buchanan and his wife, Rebecca (Becky) Snipes. Vance, being
unmarried, made himself to home at the Buchanan dinner table when he was
close by. Whatever the reason, she noticed he was there like as not, when they
came down the wagon road to visit.

Glancing at him now, she wondered why she hadn't given much thought to
the attention he gave to her parents, and their conversations by the fire. She was
usually helping Aunt Becky prepare a meal or keeping a young child from getting
too close to the fire, wasn't she? The plot they were talking up included her, while
her attention wandered. Too late now, she thought.

◆

Jane felt her spirits rise after their rest. The air was cool as the sun began its descent towards a western peak. She could almost taste the crisp, cool air sweeping down from the northern trail. Sitting there a few minutes she looked at her surroundings then rose and walked to the spring. Cupping her hands, she lifted water to her lips and swallowed greedily. Splashing water on her face made her gasp. She lifted her skirt and pulled her petticoat up to dry her face and hands. Lifting her eyes towards the sky, she saw the mountain peaks she was leaving behind. In her mind, she saw herself standing with her arms lifting towards their embrace.

Turning she was startled to see her husband close. "I'm anxious to get to our home, Vance. Is it far?" She walked to her horse and opened a box strapped to his back to get a fresh handkerchief. She turned back to face Vance.

Looking intently into her face for her mood, he sighed. "We should be there in time to have a light supper should we be hungry. Let's see, there's hominy grits, and we'll gather fresh eggs. I have all the staples and canned goods, a gift from Mother. Jane, my brother will have taken care of the stock if you'd like me to show you around the farm before bedtime. Tomorrow, we'll ride over and visit my parents." He moved to the horses and tightened the cinches.

"Will they like me, do you think?" Jane looked very solemn as Vance led her horse beside a rock, where she stepped up as he helped her to mount.

Blushing a little, he spoke. "I like you, Jane. I believe they will like you, too."

3

At Home

Vance Snipes had a pie safe in his home. These safes had doors with designs punched through the tin for decoration, and for air to circulate through. The doors kept the pies "safe" from the critters that might come wandering through. This pie safe is the one that Jane would have in her dining room when we were growing up. Glass replaced the decorative tin. It's in Effie's house now.

Jane and Vance rode side by side as they approached the farm. Vance was surprised to see one of his brothers walking from the house. "Well, we are being welcomed home. Howdy Tom. How are things this day?" Reaching the fenced enclosure, he dismounted and helped Jane. They stood together as Tom approached them.

Vance made the introductions and the two men began taking care of the horses. Turning them into the enclosure, they walked towards the house. His brother carried Jane's parcels and Vance held her arm. He had noticed his missing mules, and now looked at his brother and raised his brows. Tom shook his head. Knowing something wasn't right Vance said, "Jane, let me get some fresh water in the house. I know you'd like to wash up. I'll just show you to our bedroom, where you can leave your hat and such."

They entered a log house with the front room still awash with light. From the door she looked at the large fireplace on the back wall, flanked by two comfortable chairs. Sitting in a place of honor in back of the dining table was a pie safe with decorated tin doors. It was so pretty Jane walked over and opened the doors. To her delight the shelves displayed beautiful pies and a cake. She turned to Vance with a question on her lips but he just laughed. "A friend brought us these as a wedding gift." Jane thought that it must be a female friend. Now I wonder who she is?

"The bedroom is through here, Jane." Vance touched her arm as he led her toward the room opening to the left of the fireplace. "Now explore your new home while I get water." Smiling, he touched her arm again and turned towards the door.

He met his brother in the yard after getting a water bucket from the porch. They walked away from the house towards the spring. "When I came by last evening to take care of the stock, I knew something was wrong, Vance. The gate to the fence was open. I saw right away that old Jasper and Ben were gone."

Vance gasped. "My mules? I know I locked the gate as usual."

His brother nodded. "Oh, I'm sure you did. Your front door was open, too. Your things had been gone through, Vance. It was a real mess in there. It was thieves, for sure."

"I rode out fast, about five miles up the road, but didn't find a trace. You left afore dinnertime. I figure the thieves were watching your place and saw you leave. I believe they knew you were alone here. Anyways, I asked for help and no one has found them. They had a head start, I believe."

"The pies and cakes came after, I guess. You cleaned up good and I thank you. We won't tell Jane about this now. I'll wait until we are riding over to visit tomorrow. She'll feel better when she knows family is close by. Now, I need to show my wife where we keep the stores. Will you stay for some supper?"

His brother smiled and shook his head. "Best go on home and let you newly weds settle in. Congratulations, Brother!" And he walked away, taking a trail visible through the trees.

Jane walked out on the porch and waited as her husband walked towards her with a pail of water. She squared her shoulders as he approached and they turned and walked into the house together. She didn't love this man, she thought, but I can be his wife. I will!

Turning to him, she stopped "I'll try to be a good wife to you, Vance. I believe you to be a kind man, and I want to do my duty, so we will be all right. But understand that it won't be easy for me to be here, so far from my family. Now, it's so late, could we just have some apple pie and milk? I'll start cooking tomorrow." Smiling, she asked, "Are you very worried about my cooking?"

He began building a fire. "Well, Jane, you know I can build a fire but I don't know if you can cook." He looked over his shoulder. "I believe we will be all right. I find already that I like the way you sit your horse. Maybe you'll find something you like about me." Smiling, he turned back to the fire, then filled the kettle with water and swung it over the flickering flames.

◆

After "supper" Vance gave Jane a tour around their property. Dusk began to settle as they walked towards the house. Jane gazed at her new home, pleased with all that her husband had shown her.

Vance was proving to have a sense of humor; first he turned away her litany of their loveless marriage with a smile then laughed away her comments about her cooking skills. His demeanor changed at the door. His face suddenly paled. "Jane, being a husband will be new to me." Taking her hand, he spoke softly. "I so want to please you. Will you help me?" His words gave her courage, and quieted her pounding heart some as they walked through the door. Vance gently squeezed her hand before releasing it. "I know you're tired from our long day, Jane. We'll just get a good night's sleep and start being 'married folk' tomorrow. Will that be all right?"

4

Nancy and Bill Buchanan

I grew up hearing stories about Nancy Buchanan, and reading her "Life Story" that she had related to Jane. What I didn't hear about was her love story. As I learned about Bill Buchanan from his letters and Last Will and Testament, I could better understand their life together. The tintype we found in her belongings brings them to life for us.

Bill and Nancy are sitting on the porch as the afternoon turns to dusk. It had been an unseasonably warm day for this time of year. Lula was already asleep after all the excitement of company and the wedding. Joe had gone sparking. He and Emily Hollifield would probably be next to marry. A light breeze began to come in from the direction of now ominous looking clouds, giving a nip to the air.

"I remember our wedding day, Nancy. My heart is still so full of love for you." Bill turned and took her hand, so work worn, and pressed it to his lips. "I hope Jane learns to love him, as love is a precious thing for a husband and wife," he says as he presses her hand to his heart.

Nancy's eyes are warm as she looks at her husband. "Jane may come to love him as time goes by, Bill. I pray they will have a good life. Yes, a good safe life. Now I'll make us a bit of supper. Looks like rain. Come, the chill isn't good for you."

Thunder gave a growl then rumbling seemed to crawl across the sky. Cooler air was meeting with the unseasonably warm currents.

◆

The farmhouse was dark. A soft drizzle was beginning to fall. Bill and Nancy were asleep, but he wasn't quiet. He was dreaming that he was back in Virginia, behind the breastworks, with pickets (sentries) a firing. He saw his brother, Alford, sitting on the ground, leaning against a tree. Alford seemed to smile, and then looked down where blood was seeping from a hole near his middle. He held out his hand towards Bill then he slumped back, staring blindly.

Bill met his brother, George, walking through the smoke. Together they started marching towards Petersburg, walking around dead soldiers moving with maggots. With no words and unplanned, they stepped away from the war and started home. Jerking awake, Bill sat up in bed.

Nancy awakened seeing him with his hands to his face. "The dream again, Bill?" "Yes, thirty years and I still go back there." She touched his face and wiped away his tears, then tenderly took him in her arms. "You are here, Bill, with me now and evermore." Finally he slept there in her arms.

She lay listening to the wind driving rain against the window, letting her mind drift back, and she and the man in her arms were young again. They were married November 11, 1860. As the embers in the fireplace dimmed, he picked her up into his arms and carried her to the bed. He moved along side her, looking into her eyes with tenderness. He touched her face, then leaned down and pressed his lips against hers. He murmured, "You've made me so happy today. Our life will be good together, sweet Nancy."

And it was as they started their new life. They had a log house Bill and his brothers had built on the land set aside for them. With the money she had saved they bought stock: a cow, a large sow already heavy with a coming litter, an ox for plowing. Bill had a fine mare they hoped was in foal, and a pair of sheep for breeding from Bill's family. Knowing they were to be married in November, they had broken the cleared land and sowed corn in the spring, the seed a gift from her family and his. They also planted a fine kitchen garden.

Their good friends, William Byrd, and Martha Washburn, lived close by and visited them often. They were sweethearts and longed to get married, too. The problem was getting enough money in these hard times to start housekeeping. They knew it wouldn't be an easy task even then, starting a new home together, and looked to their friends as an example.

It was hard work. Their day started early and ended late but Bill and Nancy were young and strong. They worked side by side. What one didn't know about the work to be done, the other likely did. He had learned working on his father's farm. As a young girl, when her mother, Rachel McKinney Deweese, had remarried, Nancy hired to Martha Washburn's father. 'Known as a good liver,' she worked in his fields in the spring, summer, and fall. She worked in the house with his wife in the winter. It was here she and Martha became best friends.

Nancy and Bill had planted fruit trees in early fall and started digging out a small hill in the back of the house. The space would be shored up with timbers.

Shelves would be added for storing preserved goods, fruit, and potatoes. These goods were stored in the house, but now that they were married, they would need the room when a child came. They were finishing the 'apple house' as Nancy called it, before snow set in. The work they shared seemed almost piddling now, in the face of their youth, with their sweet awareness of each other, and the nights snuggled together.

Smiling, she turned to Bill, "Will you want a boy when we have a babe?" He dropped his digging tool and turned to her. "Are you with child, Nancy?" Pausing, she replied. "No, but I expect to be." Bill's color returned. "Well then, when that time comes, I'll want what the good Lord sends."

"Not yet but soon," he muttered. "My knees gave out and she was just talking." Looking at her, he saw her eyes on him. She was bent over, laughing. He shivered as if someone had walked across his grave. Please God, this happiness I would hold, he prayed.

Married only eight months, Bill left to go to war, July 4, 1861, returning only a few short days at a time in the next four years.

5

War, 1861

Our family has letters written by William A. (Bill) Buchanan to his wife, Nancy, from places of battle during his service in the Civil War. Some were copied before the faded pencil words disappeared. The letters written in ink are still legible but are in poor condition. I have copied them for this book as he wrote them.

When news reached the mountains that the southern cause would divide state from state, that war would decide the issue, no man or woman could hide from these events. Here, too, it was a house divided.

Though news was still slow reaching these mountains then, Nancy remembered well the Presidential Election of 1860. Both she and Bill had known this conflict was coming. Abraham Lincoln, the candidate of the Republicans, was elected and took office from the Democrat president, James Buchanan.

The Whig party, organized in 1834, had been western North Carolina's party until the 1850's. It stood for federal and state aid for road improvement and railroad building that this western part of the state needed. Bill hoped support for schools would happen in his lifetime.

The Whigs, however, took no stand on slavery issues in the 1850's and North Carolina leaders began leaving the party. The passage of the Kansas-Nebraska Bill gave new territories a choice to own slaves. The ensuing bloodshed helped change the Republican Party. It became pledged to slave-free territories. Abraham Lincoln inherited a nation that was pulling apart. He was firm that he would hold it together. According to history, James Buchanan was sympathetic to the southern cause, as was most of Lincoln's new Cabinet. Some southern Whigs began joining the Democrats, and some the new Republicans, as well as splinter parties. In western North Carolina people followed this pattern.

North Carolina's mountain people were dependent on no one ideology, but they had strong feelings about the country they helped to shape. There were many Union loyalists here, their sentiment so strong they petitioned North Carolina legislature to form a new county, Mitchell, separating themselves from secessionists. Mitchell County, which took some of Yancey, Watauga, Caldwell, Burke, and McDowell Counties, was formed in 1861 and was considered a Union stronghold. These Unionists drew the Lincoln Republican Party to their breasts and hold it there to this day, though it's principles have changed dramatically.

Most would say that people here with southern sentiments didn't have strong feelings about slavery, but did on the rights of North Carolina and other states to make decisions on such issues. When President Lincoln called for Federal Troops from North Carolina, a line was drawn, and families, as well as individuals in a family, chose sides.

Bill Buchanan, his family, and close friends, chose the southern cause. Some lived in what would become Mitchell, some in Yancey and some in McDowell Counties. Bill's brother Alford, and Bill's best friend, William Byrd, enlisted in May of 1861, when North Carolina seceded from the union. Bill followed in July. Bill and Alford's brother, George, enlisted in May of 1863, at age nineteen. (I recently received the information that Rachel McKinney Deweese' second husband, Alexander Lowery, served in the 35th N.C. Infantry, formed September 11, 1861. According to John McKinney, from Marion N.C., Alexander died in 1861, in Richmond, Virginia, probably from illness.)

They all went to Raleigh to be inducted. Here they were subjected to rowdy crowds trying to sway the young men to their way of thinking. Some were for preserving the union at all costs, against the secessionists. Impassioned speeches, fighting, and arguing prevailed. In spite of the sparring, most had already made up their minds, and walking into the unknown, Bill and his friends stepped forward to become part of the Confederate Army.

Nancy was expecting a child when Bill went to war. Martha Melissa was born September 8, 1861, just a few months after he left. Bill didn't want to go, but they both knew he had no choice. She had continued putting up vegetables and fruits as they matured until labor began. Even with her small frame she had no problem giving birth. Melissa was born with the help of her mother-in-law and a local mid-wife.

Nancy's own mother, Rachel, had given birth to a son about the time Nancy and Bill married. She had married Alexander Lowery in 1850, after returning to the mountains of North Carolina from Missouri, widowed by the death of her husband Lewis Deweese. In the past ten years she had given him six children: four girls, and with the last, two sons. Now we know Alexander died just a year after his last son was born.

Soon Nancy was doing her regular chores. Sometimes Bill seemed to be working beside her, but when she looked, she was alone. Her days seemed short but falling into bed, the nights lasted forever.

The rains didn't come in the fall. She carried water to the stock, but her gardens dried before she could put up her fall crop. Only Bill's letters gave nourishment to her arid world. Bill's family, and her own, gave her some sustenance, but she marked the time when she and her husband would be together again. Much later, she was glad she could not look into the future.

The baby was good company to her. She would place her in a nest of blankets and pillows and Melissa would watch while Nancy sewed or carded wool before falling asleep. There was no oil for lamps during the war (if they had any). Nancy used dried strips of bark to keep the firelight bright enough to give out light.

Portions of a letter from Bill:

Sunday Morning, Head Quarters, Evans Port, Prince Williams County, Virginia, January 26th, 1862.

Dear and Affectionate Wife,

With emotions of love and pleasure I spend the present opportunity of writing you a few lines to inform you that I am well and doing the best I can. I can say to you that I received your kind letter last evening, dated Jan. 12th. Which gave me great satisfaction to hear from you. I hope you will write as often as you can. If paper is scarce I can send you a little in letters. I can inform you that we are yet at our same post and no fighting yet. As to when our time will be out, I can only tell you what I think and hear. The Colonel told our Captain that we would be discharged in Raleigh the 8th of May and since we did not get furlough, it may be April 8th. I will tell you there is no person that knows how bad I want to get home but myself. I can inform you that I heard from Brother Alford not long ago and he was well and back with his Company. He is 10 miles above this place. His thigh is now well. I expect he will get a discharge before long. If he does I will send you money by him. I want you to get someone to put in a crop if you can. Be saving of your corn and take good care of your pigs and try to raise as many hogs as you can for they will sell high all the time. Also, send word how that cow is doing and take good care of my colt as you can for I want him to be large enough to ride against I get home. Give Miss Martha Washburn my love and best wishes and tell her that William Byrd is well and wants to see her the worst way. Tell her that I have done as I promised to take care of him as best I could. Give your Mother, Jane, and Mary (Nancy's sisters) my best respects and tell them I have not forgot them and never will. Write soon and take good care of the baby and send me word if it is as pretty as you say it is. I remain your affectionate husband until death.—William A. Buchanan to Nancy M. Buchanan—

HANOVER JUNCTION

Two 19th-century railroads crossed at grade level just east: the Richmond, Fredericksburg & Potomac and the Virginia Central, which ran west to the Shenandoah Valley, the Confederacy's breadbasket during the Civil War. This junction attained strategic importance in 1864 as the railroads carried supplies to Gen. Robert E. Lee's Army of Northern Virginia. Lt. Gen. Ulysses S. Grant and the Army of the Potomac attempted to disrupt that traffic to hinder Lee and capture Richmond. The Confederates, however, successfully defended the junction during the North Anna River campaign, 21-26 May 1864, and the Union army withdrew east to Cold Harbor.

Civil War Battles where William A., Alford, and George Buchanan fought. Hanover Junction.

Earth works around Hanover Junction.

Sign at North Anna Battlefield Park.

NORTH ANNA RIVER CAMPAIGN
21-26 MAY 1864

Approaching Richmond from the north after the Wilderness Campaign, Lt. General U.S. Grant sought to cross the North Anna River and capture the critical rail center at Hanover Junction (Doswell). General R. E. Lee ordered the construction of a complex web of earthworks here to defend the river crossing and junction. The Union army probed the defenses and captured some of them but soon abandoned the effort and moved east toward Cold Harbor.

North Anna Campaign sign.
Photos taken by author.

Francis Biddix, husband of Mary Deweese Biddix. Enlisted in the 58th NC
Infantry formed December 31, 1861. He was wounded,
but survived the war.

Julius A. McKinney, son of Alexander McKinney (brother to Rachel McKinney
Deweese Lowery.) Enlisted with the 58th NC on July 16, 1862.
He died 9 months later on April 18, 1863, in Knoxville, TN.

Civil War era family tintypes belonged to Nancy Deweese Buchanan and were
identified by John McKinney of Marion, NC.

Family Bible of William and Nancy Buchanan

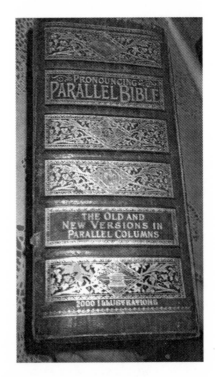

Family Bible Spine. Photos taken by Betty McKinney Mace,
daughter of Effie Snipes McKinney.

6

Virginia, 1862

My husband and I have visited some of the battlefields where William Buchanan, his brothers, Alford and George, and William's friend, William Byrd, fought. They are all around Richmond, Virginia. There are still breastworks (mounds of earth prepared by the soldiers to stand behind as they shoot) from which Bill may have written his letters to Nancy. We visited the area where the Battle of Seven Pines took place. They still uncover human remains when building roads there, as some were buried where they fell. Some bones are taken to Richmond, but there are so many. We also visited the North Anna River and Hanover Junction battlefields, the places written about in this book. These battlefields are not far apart, and battles were fought there in 1862, and again in 1864, sometimes by the same troops.

While William and Alford were in different regiments, looking at battle maps, they would sometimes be in the same battles, but separated by several miles. Circumstances and the reality of war will carve a new road where they will walk, like a sudden torrent of water veering off a known path.

Although Bill thought their enlistment was for only a year, their regiments were part of the Northern Army of Virginia, the very backbone of an army that would fight and march through four years of this war. Bill and William Byrd were in the 12th Regiment N. C. Volunteers that was organized at the fairgrounds in Raleigh on July 11, 1861. The regiment was assigned to the garrison at Evans Port, where defenses had been constructed to prevent Federal ships from navigating the Potomac River.

On November 14, 1862, this regiment was designated the 22nd Regiment N.C. troops. Later, George Buchanan would be assigned to the 22nd also, in the same Co. B as Bill and William Byrd. Alford was in Co. C, 16th N.C. Troops. Of the four soldiers, two would return to the mountains.

Bill sent a letter to his brother, George. It must have been enclosed with one to Nancy. It is evident that this is when he still thinks he will be home after his first year:

A few lines to Brother George. Dear Sir. I am well. I hope you are the same. George, I want you if you can to break up my land and plant me a crop if you can and I will pay you the money for it when I come home and I want you to write to me soon and let me know whether you can do it or not and if you can not I want to get some other person to do it for me and write to me as soon as you get this letter and do the best you can and make all you can and take good care with what you have got and do not volunteer till I come Home. So I will close and I only remain your brother until death. William A. Buchanan to Mr. George L. Buchanan. (It is likely that George did his brother's bidding, and Nancy worked the land as well.)

Bill Buchanan was wounded and William Byrd was killed at the Battle of Seven Pines, Virginia, near Richmond, in May of 1862. Bill had promised William Byrd's sweetheart that he would watch after him. He never talked about that day, even to Nancy, and to her sorrow, Martha stopped coming to visit, and just drifted away from their friendship. It's too painful for her, seeing me with Melissa, Nancy thought. Her dreams are dead on a battlefield in Virginia.

Some were buried where they fell while others were brought into Richmond, (Virginia) dead or mortally wounded. Many can be found in Richmond cemeteries. (We didn't find the names of those written about in this book except we didn't look for one likely to be there, Alexander Lowery.)

Notes from records of 22nd Regiment N. C. Troops (12th N.C. Volunteers) Official Records, S.1, Vol. XI, pt. 1, pp.990-991: This regiment was part of a movement south to below Williamsburg early in March of 1862, then onto Fredericksburg, on March 7th. (Hoping to go home in April or May they were instead moving towards battle.) *They moved to Yorktown in mid-April where they were transferred to a reserve division. Each move was under a different commanding officer until General Joseph E. Johnston was placed in command.*

Fearing the mounting Federal pressure against his defensive works, General Johnston began a general withdrawal on the night of May 3–4 towards Richmond. After discovering that two Federal Corps had crossed the Chickahominy River near the Williamsburg road in the vicinity of Seven Pines, General Johnston decided to attack the divided Federal army on May 31. This was to be coordinated with General Longstreet, General D. H. Hill, General Benjamin Huger and General Smith. Johnston's plan broke down immediately on the morning of May 31 as a result of the failure of the various commanders to reach their assigned positions and a series of piecemeal and ineffective Confederate attacks ensued.

General Smith reported the action during the battle of Seven Pines as follows: *The 22nd Regiment (12th N. C. Volunteers) did not get into action until 4:00 P.M. when it encountered the enemy on the Nine Mile Road. They were under deadly fire in a dense, entangled wood, struggling through the morass, covered with logs and thick bushes. The men somehow continued to advance without firing a shot until coming up with the front line of troops, already engaged, and they too commenced firing, advancing upon the left to within 15 to 20 yards of the line of fire of the enemy. The thickness of the woods and undergrowth and the smoke prevented them from seeing; the roar of musketry was almost deafening. Very seldom, if ever, did any troops in their first battle go so close up to covered line under so strong a fire and remain within such short distance so long a time.*

Various attempts were made to charge the enemy and many of the gallant spirits who attempted it were shot down. The troops held their positions close to the enemy's line until it was too dark to distinguish friend from foe. 147 Confederate soldiers were wounded or killed. (During this battle, General Johnston was wounded; General Gustavus W. Smith, who succeeded him, fell ill, and General Robert E. Lee was placed in command of the Army of Northern Virginia.)

◆

Nancy took Melissa to the fields in the summer, placing her under a shade tree. Working all day, she only took time away to feed her and change her diapers. She remembered coming in to milk the cow, bathing Melissa and herself, eating a meager supper, and falling into bed. Small in statue, slim and agile like a limber sapling, Nancy persevered.

One day as Nancy put Melissa to bed, a terrible storm blew up. Rain lashed the roof, and wind blew against the house. Nancy rushed out to get the pail of milk she had left on the porch. She saw a tree starting to fall on the house and hurried to get Melissa. She just had time to get her in her arms before the tree struck the house. A big limb came through the roof and the floor, a few feet from where she stood.

Nancy spent three or four days with her mother-in-law. When she came back to her house, someone had removed the tree and repaired the house. It was complete with a new lock. Nancy never knew who the 'good Samaritan' was.

Loneliness was her constant companion. One night she walked with Melissa to her sister's house to spend the night. When she came back, her house had been broken into. Someone had taken all her meat, corn, salt, and all her thread. The thread was ready to put in the loom. In her despair she wrapped what thin layer of courage she had left around her like a cloak. She would make it through, although she waited each day for news that Bill was killed.

Our Army Correspondence—From the Sixteenth Regiment

Camp Near Frederic, Maryland, September 7, 1862

Editor Asheville News:

Dear Sir: Please let these lines have room in your columns for the benefit of the friends of Company B, 16th Regt. N.C. Troops. (Alford was in Co. C. 16th Regt.). You will see by the heading that we have crossed the Potomac River, but on our march had some hard fighting. On the 29th of August our Division opened the ball at Manassas, wresting that place from the Federal forces on the 30th and 31st. The following is a list of the names of those killed and wounded: May Jervis, killed; J. W. Calloway, mortally wounded; A. Shelton, slightly in the right arm, Tim Covany, severely in the shoulder; Corp. John W. Randall slightly in left hand; Wm. Penly, slightly in leg; Thos. W. Keith, finger shot off of left hand, and First Lieut. John A. Moore, slightly in shoulder. This is the casualties in said company. The remainder of the company is on the march, and nearly worn out. We have been on the march for the last month, and there is no telling when we will call a halt. The Yankees keep moving back, and we keep on in pursuit of them, so I cannot tell when the chase will end, or what space will be run over. I have no time to write will give you more at some future time. I remain, as ever, your friend. JOHN M. CARVER, O.S.

Head Quarters 16th N. C. Troops, Camp Near Orange C. H. Va., November 29th, 1862—Editor Asheville News-The attention of the citizens of North Carolina who have friends in this Regiment is called to their destitute condition. They are greatly in need of clothing of all kinds, and especially shoes, socks and blankets. I hope they will come to our assistance. We have now before us the prospect of an active winter campaign, and your soldiers must be comfortably clothed or they cannot endure the hardships before us. We have tonight completed a march of eight days, through the most mountainous portion of Virginia, and a great many of the members of this Regiment, as well as others, have marched the entire distance barefooted. I hope the good citizens of the

**Old North State will not suffer this state of things to exist much longer.
J. S. McElroy, Col. 16th N. C. Troops**

Bill came home when he was able, and stayed until he was well enough to go back. While he was home in August of 1863, Nancy became pregnant. A son was born to them May 29, 1864. They named him Alford, after Bill's brother. He would be called Bud. Bill's brother, Alford Buchanan, was wounded several times in the first years of the war and was killed at the North Anna River, Virginia, May 23, 1864, six days before his namesake was born.

Letters from line of battle:

May 26, 1864, Line of Battle, near Hanover Junction, Virginia (approaching Richmond)

Dear and affectionate Wife:

I spend the present opportunity of writing you a short letter that will inform you I am not well, but so I can be about. I hope these lines will safely reach you and find you well and doing well. I can say to you that I have been absent from my company the past five days. By flanking the enemy I was able to get back to my company. I just got up this morning. Both armies have come from Spotsylvania and made a stand near Hanover Junction. We are now in line of battle in our breastworks waiting for Yankees to attack us, the pickets a firing. I should not be surprised at any time to be attacked. Dear Wife, there is nothing but trouble to write you about. But you must take things the best you can and do the best you can. It has pleased God to spare my life till now and I hope and pray to live through this troublesome war. Your affectionate husband, William A. Buchanan.

A poem or song is written on the back of this letter. We assume Bill wrote it.

1. **In slumbering sleep I lay one night upon my bed. A vision very strange or a thought come in my head.**

2. **I dreamed of the day of doom and doubted it had come. And Christ himself was there for to summon old and young.**

3. **And I myself was called with trumpet loud and shrill. Saying every soul must ride be their sentence good or ill.**

4.   **With fear and trembling stood. And little did I know but I knew Christ mercies great. And I trusted and did you.**

5.   **I had not been there long before old Satan came drest up in his filthy robe and my sins be brought along.**

6.   **He laid them down before the lord and said I was his own. My sins being full and great for was many I had done.**

7.   **Then said our blessed savior I soon will end the strife. I'll see if the sinners name is not in the book of life.**

8.   **The Book of Life was brought and my leaves unfold. And the sinners name was there and the letters wrote with gold.**

9.   **Then said our blessed Savior, O stay old Satan stay for the sinners name is here and his sins are washed away**

Date and place written unknown: *Dear Nancy, When our regiment started on the march, I was not able to keep up with it, and the boys thought and wrote that I was a prisoner, but by flanking I got out safe, though I was near in the hands of the enemy. I am now with my camp again and I shall take the best care of myself that I can and will keep out of all danger that I can, so do not be uneasy about me. I will do the best I can. Be sure and write me and let me know how you are getting along. How are you making out for something to eat? Send me word if you have got in a crop or not. Be sure and write soon and let Mother see this letter. I will have to close as it is going to rain. Brother George is in Richmond doing well. So no more, only I remain as ever your affectionate husband till death. William A. Buchanan.*

Near Mechanicsville VA, May 29th, 1864

Dear Wife,

With pleasure I seat myself this morning to write you a few lines to let you know that I am still in the land of the living though I have been very much fatigued and worn out owing to a long march and fighting. We have been marching and fighting about 25 days and from appearances it is not done with yet. The army is all moving down near Richmond where I look for some more hard fighting. We are now 8 or 10 miles from Richmond. I think the army will go very near there before the battle is ended. I hope will be very soon.(Continuation of letter, probably after a time lapse.) I am sorry to inform you that brother

Alford was killed last Monday in the fight that took place near here. I was not in that battle myself, but I suppose he was shot through. The ball struck him about the waist. Button, and one of his Company cut off his things, and he said to raise him up, then he dropped off, they said, like a man going to sleep. I will close as I have no good news much to write since the fighting because we have had 12 wounded and 1 killed and several taken prisoner. You must excuse my short letter, I will write again soon. Until soon, your husband, W. A. Buchanan

We can't imagine the horror and deprivation these men (and sometimes women) knew for these four, long years. Bill would have known of the hardships his wife and family were suffering at home, but was helpless to help them. When he came home their youth and his health were gone.

7

Rachel McKinney Deweese Lowery, Grassy Creek N.C., 1898

My family has stories about some of Rachel and Louis Deweese' life near St. Louis, Missouri, and Rachel's travels back to North Carolina. We have the stories, written in Grandmother Jane's hand, as Nancy related it to her when she was 84 years old. According to Nancy, she and her sisters, Mary Elizabeth (Biddix), and Jane (Washburn), were born in Missouri.

The story she told about the Indian family is different from my account. According to Nancy, they asked Rachel if she could go home with them, to play. They assured Rachel that they would bring her back home. My thoughts took a different route, as you will see.

Joe was up early taking care of the stock, milking, and tending to the minimum chores. Nancy fed and tended to Lula as Bill and Joe ate breakfast. "Bill, would you take the buggy to church and go by Mother's? She wasn't able to come for Jane's wedding, and I know she'll be anxious to hear the news. Tell her I would like her to stay a while."

Their church first met in the front room of Uncle Johnny and Aunt Patty Collis. A building was built quite a few years ago by the church founders themselves. A history, written by Carrie Washburn, was published in the *Tri-County News*, Spruce Pine, N.C., November 6, 1975 edition. According to the article, *"Johnny Collis gave the community a plot of ground on top of what was later known as the D. D. Collis Gap on the present Emerald Mine Road, to build a church. On this mountaintop was a grove of huge chestnut trees."*

"The members selected which chestnut trees to cut and with donated trees, oxen, and labor, built their church without money." This building Bill Buchanan was going to in the year of *1898 "was a one-room log cabin, dabbed with red clay with puncheon interior walls and floor, with a large fireplace made of native stone and*

clay. The seats were still split logs with pegged legs and no backs. Windows were shutters and opened for light. The roof was hand-split shingles. Tallow candles and torches were used for night-lights." It was named *Chestnut Grove Baptist Church.* The members were now talking of building a new church, hopefully by the year 1900.

Bill was already humming the songs they would be singing today. He led the singing and Jane's alto voice would be missed as she would be missed in this house.

Nancy's mother, Rachel McKinney Deweese Lowery, lives on Pepper's Creek in McDowell County, on land her daddy, Charles McKinney, gave to her. She had purchased 50 acres after returning from St. Louis, and Charles McKinney gave her 100 acres (N.C. Records). One of the stories remembered about Rachel tells of her having a long leather purse, filled with gold coins, when she returned to North Carolina.

The Yellow Mountain Road that came by Pepper's Ridge and close by her home *"came west from Morganton across the end of Linville Mountain, followed the North Fork of Catawba River to Pepper's Ridge, then swung up the mountain through McKinney's Gap into the valley of the North Toe River. It followed to the headwaters of this stream, crossing the state line over the Unaka range, between Roan Mountain and the Yellow Mountain, it descended to the Watauga River and the pioneer rallying point of Sycamore Shoals."* (From *Blue Ridge Parkway Guide* by William G. Lord, *Grandfather Mountain to Great Smoky Mountain NP, McKinney Gap.*) Mountain men from Sycamore Shoals had marched this road to their destiny at Kings Mountain, in the war that severed these colonials from Britain's rule.

Rachel is now 84 years old in 1898 and still lively. After being widowed twice she was left to raise her families alone. She expected them to come and sit and bring her all the news. Nancy hoped she would agree to come here for a visit.

Bill and Rachel arrived for the evening meal. She walked into the dim room where a lamp shed its light on a large table, and lifted a cloth from the food, ready to serve. "Wasn't surprised to see Bill. I had my things ready to go since I knew you'd be lonesome. I reckon my Jane is married up and already wife to Mr. Snipes." She catches Bill Buchanan's eye. Nancy smiled recognizing that her mother would take over the household and lead their lives while she stayed with them.

"I remember my daddy when I married up. He said 'of all my children, I will miss you, Rachel. You see I love you, and you're so like your mother.' Course, Mr. Deweese was taking me all the way to Missouri. Jane is only down the mountain a little ways."

Nancy finished laying the plates and eating utensils, and Rachel poured cool buttermilk into glasses. They sat and Bill prayed over the food. Nancy looked up. "I remember Missouri, Mother, and I remember Daddy on his deathbed."

Rachel nodded. "It started as a good life, though the winters were mighty cold. Your pa took sick, and it was all for naught." Rachel looked at Nancy. "You can plan and work hard, but only the good Lord knows what's coming."

Rachel McKinney met Louis Deweese when he came over from Big Ivy (now Madison County) to cut timber. She sees him standing on the hill, his ax resting on his strong shoulder. She had walked toward him as if he was a magnet drawing her iron will to his metal. Louis had plans to go west to take advantage of the need for timber in the growing settlements in Missouri. It had been a state since 1821. His ambition appealed to Rachel, as well as his determination to have her for his wife.

They married and left the mountains of North Carolina to homestead near St. Louis, Missouri around 1838. They traveled the Wilderness Road through the Cumberland Gap with Louis' brother and his family, and settled close by to each other.

Lumbering wouldn't be an option since the forests were already cut across the wide Mississippi River. In addition to farming, Louis took a job as peace officer. Nancy and her two sisters, Mary Elizabeth, and Jane, were born in Missouri. When Louis died there, Nancy was five years old. Rachel and her brother-in-law sold out and brought their families back to the mountains of North Carolina. They traveled by wagon for three, hard, months.

Rachel's dark eyes begin to gleam with mischief. "I've heard there're thieves about Bill. Have you heard? Likely they won't come to my house, knowing I keep my gun primed. No, I reckon they heard about Rachel McKinney Deweese Lowery. My daddy, Charlie 'Kinney, taught me to shoot. Reckon them Missouri Indians would've asked you to go home with them, Nancy, if they knew about my sharp shooting?"

Nancy still remembers the spring day the Indian family came by their homestead outside St. Louis. It wasn't unusual to see groups of them that time of year. After a cold winter with little food, their plight was apparent to the settlers there. Rachel and Nancy carried cold biscuits, left from breakfast, to the hungry children. Rachel showed them to the spring for water, and she and her three daughters sat on the stoop while the Indians ate.

A young Indian boy sat a short distance from the rest. He took a biscuit and watched Nancy as she sat in the sun. Almost five years old, she had sparkling brown eyes, and her pretty face was framed with hair almost a roan color. The boy, not long from his mother's tent, spoke to his father in a soft voice. As part of his new status as a young Indian brave, he was already thinking of one he could take as wife when she reached puberty. The older man looked at Nancy, too, and nodded to his son.

When the food was finished, the woman came to Rachel and gestured her thanks for her family's food. The older man walked to his wife and spoke to her. She turned to Rachel, pointed at Nancy, and then to her group. She was asking for Nancy. Quickly Rachel put her arms around Nancy and shook her head, no. No, they couldn't have Nancy.

"Now, I wonder what my life would've been like if I had gone along with that handsome Indian boy? Laughing slyly, Nancy looked at her husband. "Why Bill, you and I would never have met."

Her husband, leaning close, placed his cheek against hers and spoke softly. "Nancy, I would have gone west and rode on until I found you. Don't you know that?"

"Well, you and Bill did all right even though your times were hard. The terrible war, children left crippled, and some dying from fever." Rachel looks pensive. "Somehow I always thought the Lord was good to you two, though, being together all these years. I saw how you love each other."

8

Charlie McKinney, Blue Ridge Mountains, 1800

I have used the stories about Charles McKinney that were passed down orally by his families. Several were included in Estelena Harper's first book about him. None involve his father (or siblings). Nancy Melissa Buchanan was Rachel McKinney and Louis Deweese' daughter. Rachel was the daughter of Charles McKinney and his wife Elizabeth Lowery.

Lying in bed that night, Rachel's mind turned to her husbands. She had thought that her love for Louis Deweese and grief at his death would keep her a widow, but time and Alexander Lowery changed that notion. He had sized her for his bed like a carpenter measuring his first timber for their house. His youth wasn't daunted by her experience and years. He measured her by her strong body and sparkling eyes; her three beautiful daughters spoke of her fertility, and it didn't hurt that her daddy was Charles McKinney. Rachel looked straight into his eyes and decided she could give him a family and hold him to her side with her woman's vigor. They would have ten years together and she would give him six children.

Her thoughts turned then to her daddy, Charlie McKinney. She saw him young and strong again. She barely remembered her mother's face, but her father was a familiar figure in her life. His strong, lean face changed through the years. Faint laugh lines deepened, and then were covered by a bushy gray beard, but his bright blue eyes commanded the world he lived in until he closed them the last time.

When she and her brother, Alexander, were young children, he would talk about their mother, Elizabeth Lowery. She had died from a lingering illness after Alexander's birth. Milk fever, some said, had finally taken her. In his soft Scot's burr (probably spoken as he grew up in a closed environment), he talked about her beauty, both physical and in spirit, he insisted. "She was far above me in station," he said, "but she would have me, and her daddy finally agreed. She understood that I wanted to make a place for us far away from what she was used to. These mountains, though, would be her gravestones."

Charles McKinney was listed in the census of 1800 here along the Blue Ridge. He may have settled his widowed mother and siblings here when he had built a cabin. We know that he married Elizabeth Lowery March 7, 1813 (N.C. Records). The place where he settled would be noted as McKinney Gap by 1846.

Most gaps (passes) were known by the 1700's although the naming would come later. *"In the late 1600's, few passes cut through the Appalachians, and these were obscured by the dense growth of pines and hardwoods which covered the face of colonial America. And though they were known to the Indians, who found them by observing the course, which eagles followed across the mountains, the white men were slow to find these gaps."* From *The Great Wagon Road*, by Parke Rouse, Jr.

The story was that Charles first came down from Virginia with a load of apple saplings, selling them as he came to settlements. He would have come down the Wilderness Road, which branched off the Great Philadelphia Wagon Road, below Fincastle, Virginia. This was the road that brought a stream of settlers from Pennsylvania, down through Maryland, to Virginia, and the Carolinas.

Coming from the east, the passage through the mountains brought him to a height where the peaks fell away beneath his feet. Looking north and south, a ridge of mountains ran as far as he could see. Seeing the beauty of the land surrounded by high, blue-green mountains, and the bountiful game, he must have decided to try to settle here. When he came back he had his first hundred acres of land spreading out from the passage that would later be named for him.

Another story is told that Charles spent his first winter here sleeping in a hollow log. He must have worked clearing land and splitting the trees, readying to build his first cabin, when winter blew in. He would have killed game, cooking it over an open fire, rolling into a rug or blanket beside his fire when night came. Then as snow or sleet came in he would retire to his dark, coffin-like bed, cocooned like the hibernating animal he now became.

Charles' life direction was shaped by the aftermath of the American Revolution. Little is known of his life in Virginia. One story has him going back to a church service where he notices a young girl. He seeks her out and asks who her father might be. "You look so much like my mother," he told her. She replied. "My mam's dead but I've been told my pa's name was Charles McKinney." The story is that he gave her what money he had on him and turned away.

Charles' father could have been a British soldier from the highlands of Scotland, or maybe he came here as an indentured man some years before. It wasn't unusual for Scots to volunteer in the British army that had controlled their beloved country with an iron hand for the years since Culloden. They were paid a bounty to join up and this they usually gave to their poverty-stricken parents. The soldiers were outfitted with required clothing and given regular meals. Pay issued to them each two months gave reason to volunteer. Maybe he joined knowing he would be sent to the colonies, a place for new beginnings.

He could have been shipped out to the new world as punishment after the failed Highland uprising at Culloden. These men had to take an oath to King and England or die. When the colonist's began their rebellion here some stayed loyal to England and some fought for independence.

Charles' father likely would have told his family of the lands and home he left behind. The high fells reached to the sky, with the blue lochs grasping their base. There was an abundance of game and fish, but the wealthy British landowners kept the crofters from sharing in this bounty.

He might have told of the battle at Culloden in April of 1746. The Jacobite sympathizers were shot where they stood by the British, while trying to put the Catholic, Charles Stuart, on the throne of Scotland. Many highlanders were executed and their families left to starve. The King's men played Catholics against the Protestant Church of England, strangling the life's blood from the people. Children growing up in this aftermath were given memories of the bloodshed, and experienced the continuing hardships.

Living in Southwestern Virginia, the McKinney family would have had many hardships. Here a few families were settling, and mostly they stayed close together for fear of the Indians. The looming Blue Ridge sheltered these settlers, while the Indians gained sanctuary after their raiding in the Alleghenies. Few colonials were settled across these mountains yet.

"Of all the mountain ranges the Indians called the Appalachians, the Blue Ridge is the oldest and most serene. Formed 200 million years ago, it has been weathered and softened by time. So gently does the Piedmont ascend to it that it hardly seems to justify the heroic name "mountain." Beyond, in the blue haze to the west, lie newer and more rugged chains like the Alleghenies and the Cumberlands. Between these ranges—called "Old Appalachia" and "New Appalachia"—lies the Great Appalachian Valley, whose northern end is called the Shenandoah and whose southwestern end becomes Tennessee. The green Eden this encompassed is called the Valley of Virginia." From *The Great Wagon Road,* by Parke Rouse, Jr.

When Charles settled in the mountains of North Carolina the Indians of the area were sometimes a threat, as well as the wild animals searching for sustenance. This was a wilderness, their home, and it was uncertain whether the Indians, the wild animals, or Charles, would win out here. Charles would make choices that set him apart from his peers. Some people of his time could think them sinful and against God's teachings. He chose a new mother for Rachel and Alexander but didn't marry her. Some said she was Elizabeth's sister. He brought her to his home and worked hard adding to his holdings, in spite of hardships and gathering trouble.

It might be that other people settled close by his land, so that he could go trapping or hunting for some days, without leaving his family without help. However it happened, it was heard that he came upon young women from time to time, whose husbands had gone off and never returned, likely killed by Indians or wild animals. Some had young children, but all were hungry and terrified to be alone in the wilderness. He brought them back to his settlement. How could he leave them, remembering his sweet Elizabeth, bringing her so far away from her folks only to die in this lonely place? But not alone, he must have thought, never alone.

His settlement grew, now with four families, each in their own home. It was told that he spent a day or two with each family, making sure that all was well with each household. One tale was told of a black "painter" (cougar?) coming to one home in the dead of night. The woman and her children were alone when they heard a screaming call close by. She knew the cry of a panther, and made sure the door was bolted and quickly closed the shutters on each window. She heard the cat scrambling on the roof. She feared it could find the opening of the chimney. Taking the gun and powder horn hanging over the door she prepared the gun, and lying on the floor before the fireplace, put the barrel up the chimney and fired. Luckily Charles was staying in a house close by and came to their rescue. He shot the panther with the aid of light from the moon and starlight.

How it came about that he acted as husband to four wives (or whether he did), Rachel will never know. She did know that it's told they bore his children and she and Alexander had many half brothers and sisters. He was well respected by the other settlers, though. Rachel was proud to be part of his legacy—one that had become legendary now.

An old, brittle daybook, titled *Jacob Carpenter's journal of obituaries*, has survived to this day. It was begun in 1841 and had this about Charles McKinney: *"Charley 'Kiney, age 72, died May 10, 1852. Was farmer, lived in mountains on Blue Ridge at 'Kiney Gap. He had four women, course married to one. Rest lived on farm. All went to crib for their bread; all went to smoke house for their meat. He killed about 75 to 80 hogs every year. Women never had words about him having so many women. This time would be hair pulled. There were 42 children belonging to him. All went to preaching together, nothing said these days. Everybody go along smooth, help one another. He made brandy all of his life. Never had any foes and got along smooth with everybody. I knew him.* " (I have assisted the reader by correcting Mr. Carpenter's spelling.)

Although her daddy had been gone for many years, Rachel still held him close to her heart. His courage in his way of life was a part of her. She hoped that she had passed it on to her children and grandchildren. Time would tell.

9

Jane Buchanan Snipes, McDowell County, 1898

The newly married couple began to settle into their new life. It was daunting to have the entire household to see to. Her first washday was a trial. She and Vance carried water to the pots, one for washing, and one for rinsing. She noticed that Vance's movements tended to slow by midday. Remembering her daddy's frailness, she worried.

Surprisingly, she easily accepted Vance as a close companion as the two of them took care of their household and farm. Their intimacy was a shock but became easier, too. She accepted it as part of this new relationship. In spite of his companionship, however, she missed her family and friends. She was lonely.

Jane churned fresh cream into butter and tried her hand at making cottage cheese using her mother's recipe. Vance complimented her cooking even before the dishes became more palatable. She began to believe that she could do no wrong in his eyes. He cared for her and she was saddened when she couldn't feel more than friendship.

Jane was sweeping the porch one morning when a wagon pulled into the yard and stopped close to the front door. Vance grinned. "Well, my surprise is here. Let's see if you like it." They walked up to the wagon and looked at a large, wood burning cook stove, complete with warming closets above the cooking surface and an oven below. Even though her mother still cooked on the fireplace, Jane certainly knew about these stoves. The problem was, she had never used one.

Vance and the driver wrestled the stove to the edge of the wagon. The driver was tall and must have weighed two hundred and fifty pounds. He jumped to the ground and told Vance to push the stove. As it cleared the wagon he took the stove in his arms and set it on the ground. Jane looked on with wide eyes.

Vance was just as awe struck as the man picked up the stove, carried it up the steps, and started towards the door. Jane moved out of the way as Vance followed him inside. He directed him to the new kitchen, while Jane looked on.

The man turned to them, grinning. "I wrestle bears in my off time from the store. This here stove lifting keeps my strength up." With that comment he went out the door and climbed into his wagon. Turning, he waved as he drove his team towards the road.

"Well, that's our entertainment for a while. I didn't know the price included a bear wrestler. I wonder if he's just pulling our leg? My sister bought her stove from him, Jane. She can give you some pointers about cooking on it when she comes for a visit. Do you like it?" Vance looked a little worried.

Jane smiled. "Thank you, Vance. I do like it. Let's hope it will like me. You may have to wait breakfast now, until I get the knack. Oh, I'll just use the fireplace and the stove. That may be better." She knew she was just babbling, but her talk was making her feel better.

"I'll be going to look at new mules tomorrow. I want them to be used to me before I break up the garden in the spring." Jane looked around, her face bleak. "Mother and sister are coming for a visit tomorrow. I'll be back long before they tell you all their gossip. Don't fret, Jane," he said, looking contrite. "I didn't tell you before, because I didn't know if I could get away."

"Thank you for telling me that, Vance. I know you're thoughtful of my feelings and I appreciate that." She ducked her head and then spoke. "I'm looking forward to tomorrow, visiting with your mother."

Jane's thoughts turned to the times her family and neighbors had gone to Marion to sell vegetables and what not. The mountain people would load a wagon with goods they would sell or trade for whatever they might need for the coming winter. After traveling the afternoon, they camped for the night, and then rose early to begin selling their produce and such. It had been a time of good fun around the campfires: visiting, story telling, and listening to music.

"Vance, could we go to the nearest town sometime? Would that be Marion? When we can, I would like to buy cloth for your shirts and maybe a dress for me." She still shivered when she thought of the strangers taking Vance's mules and most of his clothes.

"Well, we can go and I planned on that. I expect we can take a wagonload of goods to sell." He grinned like a schoolboy. "You might want to look for a new book. Would you like that, Jane?"

She laughed, almost giddy thinking of it. "Be sure and tell me in plenty of time and I'll be ready." Her thoughts were warm towards her husband. He is so good to me, she thought. I don't feel romantic love for him but his gentleness and kind heart is almost enough.

Jane found that she was expecting a child. She prayed the baby would be born healthy. He or she would be company to a life that was becoming so lonely. Loneliness and anxiety about her daddy's health dragged on her.

♦

Vance and Jane did go back up the mountain, just as the leaves on the trees were unfurled. They left home early in the morning. They were soon enshrouded in the fog as they ascended the trail. This was a remembered world.

Her heart beating fast with excitement, Jane leaned over her horse's neck and hugged him. "Oh, what a wondrous place. See the shades of green that color the leaves through the mist, Vance? Ah, my heart clutches at the sight!" Vance turned. "Do you miss it so much now, Jane?" Contrite, she smiled. "Yes, but we have a home now, Vance. As I remember you telling me, don't fret, everything will be all right." Smiling, they both turned to share the view.

Suddenly a buck deer bolted across their path trailing blood. It stumbled and fell against a fallen log. Vance jumped from his horse, lifting his gun. He aimed and shot the deer where he lay. "Jane, we need to dress this deer. Your parents will be glad to have venison this time of year. If his shooter shows up, we'll share."

Jane knew her parents usually had lamb on their menu in the spring but venison could be shared. Sometime later they rode onto Buchanan land with the deer carcass tied across the back of Vance's horse. Jane's heart skittered as they rode their horses to the gate of her parent's home.

"Jane, go to the house. I know you want to see them. I'll take care of the horses. Tell your dad that we have venison to see to." With that comment Jane dismounted, and ran to meet her mother and daddy as they came out on the porch. They both folded her into their arms. Jane noticed their grief stricken faces. They told her that sweet Bud had passed away.

They sat on the porch and told her about dressing her dear brother's frail body for his last journey, and the terrible image of the Elliotts loading Sallie Ann and the children in their wagon. They were taking them away from their home.

(Sallie Ann was expecting a child when Bud died. Their daughter was born July 4, 1898, and was named Alford Anna according to Nancy Buchanan's family bible. It isn't known if Bud had chosen this name before he died, but it is likely that he did. Alford Buchanan, his uncle for whom Bud was named, was killed at the battle of The North Anna River during the War. This name would be a heavy burden for a child to carry. She became known as Freddie. Her family spelled her name Alfred (although Bill spelled his brother's name Alford in his letters) and her nickname came from this spelling. Freddie married Salve McKinney. They are buried at the Burnette Cemetery close by Chestnut Grove Church, with a headstone showing her name as Annie B. McKinney.)

Vance heard most of the details when he walked onto the porch and Bill stood and motioned him into the house. "Come, Vance, you need to wash up, then we can take care of the deer. Nancy, if you have boiling water, we'll take it out back and get the venison ready for hanging." Bill and Vance walked into the house and back out with the kettle

Nancy stood and held out her hands to Jane. "Lula will want to see you now. She is frail today and won't come to the porch."

As Jane started forward she saw Bud's little Maude, peeking out from behind Nancy's skirts. Nancy was helping with the children, with Sallie Ann expecting a baby, and being a new widow. She knew that her mother would keep Maude if she could.

They walked into the dim room to Lula's bed. She tried to hold her arms out to Jane. Jane looked at Nancy with alarm feeling Lula's frail body. How long could this delicate child-woman hold on? Looking at her mother, Jane wiped away tears. "I feel so guilty, leaving her. I'm afraid she's given up, Mother."

Nancy patted Lula and looked at her tall, healthy daughter. "We all love her very much but we love you, too. She knows you needed to start your own home. She may be sad you are gone but I believe she understands." Looking at Lula, she thought she saw agreement in her eyes, or maybe she wanted to see it so badly it was there.

Sitting at the table after supper, Vance cleared his throat. "Jane and I have news. We are to have a baby sometime in late January or early February. We will need you both to help us nurture this new life."

Bill looked into Nancy's eyes. Tears welled and spilled down his cheeks. With a practiced hand she reached up, wiped them, and then brought his hand to her face. "Bill and I have shared these wonders these many years, Vance. May God give us the time to share yours."

While it was still light, Jane and Vance walked to her grandmother's house and took prepared food for the next day. Now that Elizabeth and Sarah were both frail they didn't do much cooking. Joe kept their fires going. The two houses were close enough that Nancy, Bill, and Joe, could go regularly to visit and help out. This was one reason that Bill and Nancy had decided to build on their land here. That and the fact that Dock and Melissa had their homes close by. Elizabeth and Sarah loved for Jane to read to them from their Bible. This time they received the news of the baby and couldn't stop talking about this coming event.

In the night, Jane lay awake beside Vance in the little attic room, thinking of her life. Her last night here, fear of leaving the safety of this home had overwhelmed her. Tonight she had her own home and would soon have a child. She shivered, thinking that she and Vance were now a part of life's cycle. Death would always come but she wouldn't think about it now. She would think of birth and life. This thought gave her peace and she slept.

They went to church the next day, leaving Joe to stay with Lula. Jane hadn't seen her friends and family since her wedding, so everyone came to them teasing and joking about her married state.

Tom and Fons McKinney, sons of Robert and Susie, came over to pay their respects and Jane introduced them to Vance. Fons looked so intently at Jane that she blushed. She passed it off as just teasing from a young boy. He did look older than he was and she noticed that the girls were paying particular attention to him. Although they lived down the hill from her parent's home, the young boys were busy with chores and had adventures of their own. She recognized them, but didn't know much about Robert and Susie's family.

10

Cycle Of Life

Vance had spent the morning cutting hay. Jane had dinner ready when he came home. She had prepared October beans from last years crop, steamed young cabbage, fried apples, buttermilk and cornbread. She was proficient on her cook stove by now, enjoying the convenience. Vance sighed with pleasure. "Jane, you are a wonderful cook. I'm a lucky man!"

With a sad expression on her face, Jane turned to him. "Thank you. I was hoping to entice you with food."

Vance's eyes widened. "Why, Jane, you surprise me. What could I, a simple man, offer up to you?"

Jane lowered her head and whispered. "I need to visit Mother and Daddy, Vance. Your brother brought a letter today. Daddy isn't well."

Shocked, Vance leaned close to Jane and took her hand. He pressed it to his face. "We will go. Let me make arrangements for the animals and we'll leave right away. Do you feel well enough to ride or should we take the buggy?" They left on horseback, as Jane took every opportunity to have the freedom of riding

Her thoughts were on their destination as they rode up the mountain, on her daddy. She couldn't give up her daddy. Please, Lord, don't take him yet, she prayed. Taking both hands from the reins, she rubbed her face then quickly gathered them again before her mount could take control. Vance rode close and spoke quietly to her, reaching to touch her arm, hoping to calm her.

They arrived to see Nancy, Maude, and Lula, sitting on the porch. Lula sat in a rocker with a soft sheet tied around her, keeping her upright. Nancy stood and put her arms around Jane as she and Vance stepped onto the porch. "He's resting. I believe he is some better today. Bill is beginning to fail I think. The doctor thinks it's his heart. His health and stamina were gone when he came back from the war. I pray he has some years with me yet. I pray."

Jane walked through the door and close to her father's bed. His eyes were closed, but he opened them when he felt her presence. Opening his arms to her, Jane sat down and let him hold her close.

"I'm all right, Jane, truly. I'm afraid I scared Nancy when my strength just seemed to go, but I've been up today, and I feel stronger. Now let me get up. If I'm to live I need to keep my blood moving." He gave a soft laugh and swung his legs to the floor, sat for a minute and got to his feet. Jane took his arm and they walked to the porch to join the family. Soon Nancy, Jane, and Vance walked over to Granny Buchanan's house for a visit.

Later Bill led Jane and Vance to the barn, where he had stored a beautiful rocking chair he had lovingly built. "Nancy and I want you to have this. We'll get Joe to bring it down. I believe we'll be able to come, too, before cold weather sets in."

◆

The winter was harsh. Hog killing was a Snipes family affair. It helped Jane that all the women and men worked up the meat then shared it. Snow began in November and sometimes drifted up past the windows. Jane and Vance were prepared with plenty of wood and food, but he had to dig a path to the barn and chickens. Some of the chickens froze and Jane made chicken and dumplings, chicken pie, and chicken soup. She and Vance laughed, saying that they would be cackling before spring. She kept busy making baby clothes. Her tiny stitches and tucks had Vance watching her nimble fingers. His tender glances spoke of his deep feelings for her and the coming baby.

Jane began labor on the twelfth of February. The weather had broken so the mid-wife attended. She was a black mid-wife from South Carolina who had come this far north after the war. Old and wizened, she took charge of the labor and Vance. She brought him into the birthing room when Jane's contractions were close and she was limp with fatigue. He sat in a straight chair and the mid-wife got a protesting Jane out of the bed. She directed Jane to rest on Vance's lap and squatted in front of them. A gush of blood and water came, and then the next contraction brought the head of the baby. Telling Jane to push hard, the next contraction brought a beautiful baby girl into the waiting woman's hands. They named her Effa (Effie) Louisa.

(Jane was an avid reader. She probably read most of Louisa May Alcott's books and may have decided to name her daughter after this favorite author. I wonder if Jo from *Little Women* might have been her favorite character. I would love to know what my grandmother felt about her woman's place in the world she knew in the years approaching the 20th century.)

The mid-wife bringing Vance into the room and having him physically part of the birth seems unusual for the times. We can't know her motive just that Vance did what she asked of him. (No one who knows this story mentions that it could have been Vance's idea to hold Jane as she delivered his child.)

Vance's mother came to help out. Jane felt loved and cared for. Effie gave her delight snuggled to her breast to suckle. Jane bathed her in front of the fire and watched her little fists and feet as she punched and kicked in the warm room. Then she would lay her in the cradle and rock her to sleep. She, Effie, and Vance, began to bask in their world here in this haven from the cold winter, but spring would bring changes Jane didn't anticipate.

11

Moving Into The 20TH Century, 1900

The men shot their rifles and lifted jugs of homemade brandy to celebrate the new millennium. Here in the mountains expectations for the future were usually limited to good weather for crops and animals and good health for their children. Jane's young family stepped into this new century hoping for these blessings, too.

Little Effie was leaving her quilt to scoot around the wood floor and pull up on her daddy's legs or her mother's long skirts. Last year she had cooed and cackled to her grandparents as they paid court to their youngest grandchild. Nancy and Bill Buchanan came for several visits during the summer and fall while Melissa cared for Lula. Jane and Vance were able to go about their many duties on the farm since their child had plenty of attention.

Nancy brought the news that Robert and Susan McKinney had sold their place to her brother and bought land around Chestnut Grove, close by Stephen Collis. "Robert plans to build a gristmill on a right swift stream on his land. The boys helped Robert build a cabin. It'll be lonesome with the McKinney boys gone."

Vance's parents became ill in the spring and Jane visited her in-laws often. Uncle Bob, Aunt Becky, and all the family cared for Mr. and Mrs. Snipes, but both died within days of each other. Their passing took its toll on the Snipes family. They all came together for strength.

Jane was beginning to feel more confident with new people she met at church meetings. Her sweet alto voice added to the church singing, and all were drawn to her quiet ways and little Effie. From the outside Jane seemed serene, but gradually her inner turmoil became evident. Not able to understand her own feelings, she looked at Vance as the problem. She became critical of what she saw as his complacency: his dress, the way he wore his hair. Leaving one day to visit a friend, she told him, "Shave your mustache before I get home. It's easier to keep

your face clean that way." When she returned, he was clean-shaven. Her con-
science hurt her so bad she was especially sweet to him for days.

In the fall Jane and Vance came to help Joe, Molt Schism, and her dad,
slaughter their hogs. Jane especially wanted to learn how Nancy canned her wonderful sausage balls. During that time Jane heard that Fons McKinney had married Hattie Waycaster. She knew he was only nineteen and Hattie was younger.
Marrying this young usually meant hardship and was to be avoided if possible.
Jane didn't know if she felt happy or sad for the young couple.

Both Nancy and Bill were busy helping other Chestnut Grove Baptist Church
members plan a new church. The church was to be started on a plot of ground
donated by William Collis. Materials and labor were again to be donated. This
time the building was to be larger and have glass windows. This was a very happy
event in their community. With a new church it might be possible to get a minister to come to the community more often. Baptisms and weddings could be
planned.

Thinking of her own marriage, she realized how little she knew of marital rela-
tions. She and Vance had grown closer while waiting for Effie to be born, but
after her birth, Vance seemed to be more reserved towards Jane. Their companionship while working together was the same and they had mutual joy in Effie,
but at bedtime Vance made excuses to stay up, usually coming to bed after Jane
was asleep. She had accepted the intimacy in their marriage knowing it was
required of her. It was unsettling to realize that it had ended prior to Effie's birth
and had not begun again. She asked him if he no longer needed her in this way.

He looked at her and turned away. "Yes, I do need you, Jane," he said, and
turned to look into her eyes. "Sometimes it isn't possible to have all you want.
Will we be all right? Is this enough, Jane?"

She walked to him and looked into his eyes. Tears welled as Jane placed her
arms around him. "Yes, Vance, we will be all right." Closing her eyes her mind
wandered over the possibilities. Was he ill? Was he frightened for her because of
being part of Effie's birth? She wished they talked easily so such questions would
come naturally.

She instinctively knew that asking would bring them closer and knew she
didn't want this. I am a coward, she thought. I'm not willing to offer myself for
fear of loss. Do I embrace my fate or hold back and just watch from a safe distance?

When she was alone she knew why she felt so empty. She had Vance who
loved her and a beautiful little girl. The failure was hers.

As the spring of 1901 began, they had news that Elizabeth Buchanan and her sister, Sarah Hollifield, were near death. Jane felt shame that she couldn't be with her grandmother and aunt. These women had helped mold her and she loved them. How had she been so caught up in her own worries and forgotten that her granny was coming to the end of her life? This guilt would follow her to her own end.

◆

Sarah Hollifield died on her birthday, May 24, and Elizabeth Hollifield Buchanan died five days later on May 29, 1901. They were buried side by side in the Buchanan Cemetery. Bill Buchanan stood by his mother's grave, looking at the freshly turned earth. "I'm thankful I lived past her time, Nancy. Losing Alford in the war like she did, I vowed to be here to hold her hand as she passed to our Lord." He turned to look into her eyes. "You and I know the pain of living past our children. I pray that we won't be left again." Turning, he took her arm and they walked to the waiting buggy.

On April 10, 1901, Elizabeth Buchanan had conveyed her house and one-half of her land in Mitchell and McDowell County, to W. A. (Bill) Buchanan, for the sum of her support or maintenance during her lifetime, and also for the support or maintenance of Sarah Hollifield during her lifetime. The Registered Deed described it as one-half of all the following pieces or parcel of land designated as follows: ... *on the headwaters of Grassy Creek known as the G. R. Dale lands, conveyed by him to Elizabeth Buchanan and A. A. Buchanan (Alford, her son?). First tract beginning on ... Isaac Washburn corner, on top of the Blue Ridge in the county at the grass fence 100 poles more or less to a cherry on top of the Blue Ridge in the county line at the grass fence between G. R. Dale and R. P. McKinney (my great-grandfather), then a north-east with the grass fence 100 poles more or less to the Green, thence East with the Green, 20 poles more or less to the John Westall line, conveyed to G. R. Dale by John Westall; thence East with the Green 146 poles to a stake in Washburn's line, thence with 100 poles to the beginning. Containing 100 acres more or less. Second tract lying in McDowell County, joining same land. Beginning on a white oak on top of the Blue Ridge in the county line and runs south 15 poles to a white oak, thence north 55' east 40 poles to a stake, thence north 6 poles to a chestnut in the county line thence with the county line 40 poles to the beginning, contain 4 acres more or less. Book 59, page 34.* She and Sarah were to remain in her house until their deaths.

(I have listed the details of this property since it sounds like some of the property the Switzerland Company purchased in 1909, from Emily Buchanan, 55 acres and 4 acres. I don't know who received the other half of this property.)

During the following weeks, Bill and Nancy spent time each evening discussing the plans for their future. He brought out all the deeds for lands he had purchased through the years, spreading them under the lamplight. Looking at her, he spoke quietly about their children, stopping to listen as Nancy spoke. In agreement, Bill made plans to make his last will and testament. On July 4, 1901, he sat down with paper and pen, before his chosen witnesses, and began to write.

In the name of God, Amen

This July 4, 1901;

I, W. A. Buchanan, being in bad health but of sound mind, thank God for his blessings, and considering the uncertainty of life and certainty of death, do hereby make my last will and testament, and first of all, I commend my spirit unto God who gave it and my body to the disposal of my friends. First: I give and bequeath unto my wife, Nancy M. Buchanan, all my lands lying in Mitchell and McDowell Counties, North Carolina, except the piece or parcel of land conveyed to me by Elizabeth Buchanan, deceased, together with all the building and apurtuments thereunto belonging, to have and to hold during her lifetime for her support or maintenance during her lifetime and also for the support and maintenance of my youngest daughter, Lula Buchanan, also I give and bequeath unto my wife Nancy M. Buchanan, all my personal property, together with all farming utensils and household and kitchen furniture, second I give and bequeath unto my youngest son, Joseph N. Buchanan, the piece or parcel of land left to me by Elizabeth Buchanan, deceased, also after the death of my wife, Nancy M. Buchanan, all the lands being in Mitchell County, all property, all household and kitchen furniture to belong to my youngest son, Joseph N. Buchanan and Lula E. Buchanan, my youngest daughter and I do appoint my youngest son, executor to set the.... and take care of my youngest daughter, Lula E. Buchanan, provided she be alive at the time and at her death all her part to belong to Joseph N. Buchanan. And, also, after the death of my wife, Nancy M. Buchanan, all the lands in McDowell County known as the Buckeye Cove tract is to belong to Daniel (Dock) S. Buchanan and Mary Jane Snipes. Daniel S. Buchanan to have all the land south of a line running from a large buckeye, comes up the branch to a large cliff, and Mary Jane Snipes to have all on the north side. (We know Daniel (Dock) Buchanan as having the middle initial of L. The clerk writing this will for the record may have misread the middle initial.) *As to the other three heirs, I consider that I have given them their part when I sold them their lands. This will is not to be of any force or effect until the death of the testator. Signed in the presence of: E. A. Snipes, G. H. Dale,*

W. A. Buchanan (Seal

Nancy and Bill Buchanan hoped that with this testament they had prepared for the future.

12

McDowell County, 1903

Jane poured coffee into both cups, before returning the pot to the stove, and sat down across from her husband. "You're up before Effie this morning, Vance. Are you feeling better today?"

"I do have more energy and my head has eased." He turned and held out his arms as little Effie toddled, barefoot, into the room. With a squeal she settled into the crook of his arm then circled her arms around his neck. Jane lifted a woolen shawl from the back of her chair and leaning across the table, wrapped it snugly around her child. Could it be that she is almost three and a half years old, she thought.

Vance spooned oatmeal into Effie's mouth and looked at Jane with a smile. "The weather is fine and the signs point toward a warm spell. I thought we would go up the mountain today, and visit your mother and dad for a few days. I know Joe and Emily wanted us for their wedding last week. Maybe a visit now will make up for that."

"I would love to go, but are you sure you feel up to the trip?" Jane moved to the stove and dished up more oatmeal, adding a little honey for Vance and Effie's dish.

"We'll take the buggy and quilts to keep the chill out. Effie will like the ride and you and I need the company of your family. It's been a long winter; ice breaking down trees and more cold rain than snow. Your brother, John, is still cleaning up from the flood of '01, trying to clear the logjam where the water swept all his cut timber. He probably has trees down again this winter."

"You'll want to ride over to your brother's and see if one of his boys can take care of the stock. I'll pack our things and take care of Effie. We'll be ready by the time you get back." Jane took Effie from Vance's arms. She squirmed and twisted to get down but Jane prevailed. Taking a kettle of warmed water from the stove, she walked to a pallet before the fire, poured the water into a basin sitting on the hearth, and prepared to bathe her little girl.

Her mind skipped ahead to her former home up the mountain. Though mourning the loss of his mother, the last two years had gone well for Bill, and Nancy. Now that Joe and Emily Hollifield were married they would make their home with them. Nancy was happy that she had another daughter, Lula another sister, and she and Bill could look forward to grandchildren close enough to enjoy. Jane was more relaxed about her father's health although he seemed frail now. She was concerned about Granny Rachel. We must go to see her. She's 89 years old and still at her home, Jane worried, and remembered that she was unable to spend time with Granny Buchanan before her death.

I know Vance is not well, Jane thought, as she turned back to her situation here. It wasn't a temporary problem anymore. She shivered, remembering his headaches and lack of appetite these past months.

◆

Driving up to the Buchanan gate, Jane and Vance met the doctor carrying his medical bag. Jane's hand pressed her heart as he approached. "Is it Daddy, Doc Fairchild?"

"It's Lula, Jane. She has croup, maybe pneumonia. I've left medicine but it's in the Lord's hands now." He lifted his hat then settled it firmly on his head, and mounted a horse tied close by. According to local history, Doc Fairchild was the only person who gave medical care in the area. He rode over from Seven Mile Ridge, so served many patients.

Vance went home after a few days to take care of their stock while Jane and Effie stayed on. Emily was a great help, and with Jane and Nancy, took turns caring for Lula. Bill kept his rocker close by her bed where he could hold her hand. Little Effie would climb into his lap and lean over and pat Lula's head.

They each held her close, bringing love and comfort to this child-woman. With her family around her, she stopped breathing February 15, 1903. She was 21 years old.

Vance arrived as Bill and Joe were building Lula's casket. Looking at the beautiful wood being shaped by their hands, he saw himself being laid there. Shaking his head he picked up a planer and began smoothing the wood.

Emily came out of the house and walked over to her husband. Joe put his arms around her before leaning away and wiping the tears from her face. "Nancy and Jane are going to bathe her, Joe, and put her in that pretty dress. I couldn't stay. How can they stand up to this?"

Bill lifted his head and looked towards the house. "She died before the flowers bloomed. I always thought we'd be able to put them all around her. She was our flower, though, and her memory will never fade."

At the cemetery, as the minister said his words, and Nancy and Bill touched their youngest daughter's casket for the last time, snow began falling, kissing the wood as it was lowered into the ground. "Frozen flowers, Nancy. I knew Lula would have flowers following her to her resting-place." Taking her arm Bill walked her to the buggy.

◆

Bill began coughing the night after Lula was buried but seemed better the next day.

Stepping out into cold, Jane and Vance packed the buggy for their return home. The snow was dry and blew about with the wind. The sky was clearing but held a hard freeze. A slight breeze lifted fairy dust from the tree limbs and spiraled the sparkling frozen mist across their faces.

"I know we need to go home, Vance, but I'm worried about Daddy. I have a bad feeling." Looking at her husband, she began to tremble. He brought her into his arms and held on tightly until she eased. She pulled back and looked at him. "I see Daddy looking far away where we can't see. Is he looking at death, Vance?"

◆

In the spring of April, as the trees began sprouting many shades of green, Bill Buchanan fell ill. At first he was able to take pleasure in his children as they came to be with him. Melissa and Jane helped Nancy nurse him and could sit quietly talking to their father. John Henry, Joe, and Dock, would entertain him with stories about the times they had shared. Then he slept without resting, his breathing rough after deep coughs failed to give him relief. Today he lay taking shallow breaths while Nancy sponged his face with cool water.

"I dreamed about William Byrd, Nancy." He reached for her hand, tightening his grip until she gasped with the pain of it. "I need to tell you of that day. I thought I could take it to my grave but I need to tell it, Nancy."

Pale with perspiration shining again on his face, Bill began speaking in a soft voice. "William was so disappointed that we weren't released in spring of '62. We all were but he couldn't reconcile himself to an unknown war." He paused, his mind going back there where no one could bear to go again. "We walked together as we headed south marching from place to place, changing commanding officers as we went. Starting back north we were to meet the enemy, who ever they were, attacking near Seven Pines, approaching Richmond."

"We marched mile after mile in the rain and mud; day after day, always hungry, exhaustion is all we knew. Gunfire sounded behind and in front as our boys ahead of our line fell to their knees. Bullets hit William and me and we fell together. Our company hadn't known that we had walked straight to the front lines. My arm was around him, Nancy, when I woke. I turned my head and looked into his eyes. They stared at me without life. I held him until one of our own found us."

"I was overwhelmed with grief and shame that I was here and William had died, but I wanted to come back to you, Nancy. I have carried this guilt, surviving, but glad, glad, that I was able to come home."

Jane came into the room to relieve her mother, but stepped quietly to the porch when she saw them so intent on each other. Sitting on the steps she let the despair she felt sweep over her. My dear daddy is weaker each day. He will die, she thought, and Mother will be half a person. I will be in a world that will lack depth or color because he will be gone. She lowered her head to her lap and wept.

A few days later they got word that Sally Ann, Bud's widow, had died April 18th. She had lived five years after Bud had died with consumption. Little Maude was 10 years old and she and her siblings were orphans. She and sometimes her sister, Freddie, would live with Nancy until they married.

On April 26, his birthday, exactly 64 years since Bill Buchanan was born, he released his grip on Nancy's hand and sighed his last breath. Nancy and children stood quietly. They did not weep.

On July 6, 1903, his son and executor, Joe N. Buchanan, filed William Buchanan's "Last Will and Testament" in Superior Court.

Book II

13

Fons McKinney, Peppers Creek, McDowell County, 1904

When I was a child, my grandfather, Papa Fons, was that special man who lived with my grandmother, Granny Jane. They lived in a wonderful place: a snow covered land in winter, where Santa lived, and a summer time of sweet breezes and bountiful food. Most of what I remembered from that time was their love for me. It was only when I was growing up that I heard he was a strict father, who required his daughters to 'toe the line.' Here is how his adulthood began.

Fons, his wife Hattie (Waycaster), and little Lawrence, stand among the crowd beside Rachel McKinney Deweese Lowery's grave (Nancy Buchanan's mother). Hattie is big with child, looking too young to have a two year old and another on the way. Her light colored hair catches the sun as she leans down to say something to little Lawrence.

Fons, shorter than his wife by several inches, shows no disadvantage to his 5' 8"s and his blue eyes look over the group with assurance. One of his strong hands rests on his son's shoulder and the other is at ease by his side.

Fons had always been in awe of his great-aunt because she was the first daughter of his great-grandfather, Charles McKinney. In addition, at age 90, she was a legend in her own right. Going to Missouri with her first husband, Louis Deweese, she had brought her family back to these mountains in a wagon after his death.

She had told the children, Fons among them, her story while they all sat around the fireplace one Christmas. She told of her children's dog being left on the side of the Mississippi River, as the Deweese families started across on the flatboat. How amidst the children's cries, the dog was spotted swimming close by the flat, and the black man held out his oar to rest the dog. Fons remembered how scared they were after hearing about fierce Indians and children being buried along the trail coming back to these mountains. Now she is dead.

Looking across the open grave, he saw Jane and Vance Snipes standing beside Nancy Buchanan, who was holding little Effie's hand on one side and Maude's on the other. Jane and Fons had seen each other these past months at Rachel's home. Jane was still grieving for her daddy when she and Effie had stayed some weeks, helping to care for Rachel during her last illness. Rachel lived close by to her Lowery children and didn't lack for care, but Jane had so many happy memories of being with her grandmother and her Lowery kin. Fons came by from time-to-time to help tend her animals and the garden she loved. Sometimes he stayed for supper and enjoyed Jane's cooking.

Looking at Jane he wondered again about her marriage. All the time she was with Rachel and Vance didn't visit. Was he too sick to be a husband to her? Did she love him?

He spoke to Hattie. "Bring Lawrence and we'll pay our respects to Mrs. Buchanan." His wife was shy but knew she had better do as Fons said. Young as they were, he let her know that being her husband, he 'ruled the roost.' Taking her child's hand she walked with him to their side.

Since Effie was almost five years old, the approach of the younger boy gave her an opportunity to show off. "You're just a baby and babies don't come to funerals," she said. "She's my great-granny. Is she your great-granny?" She looked at little Lawrence who just stared and made no reply.

"Shhh, Effie." Jane leaned down to her daughter. She looked up at Hattie and smiled, then straightened. "An only child can be trying. Little Lawrence will be glad to have a brother or sister, I hope."

Hattie blushed. "We hope he will."

"How are Susan and Robert?" Nancy turned, looking for Fons' parents. They had moved away from the house below Nancy and Bill several years ago. The little boys they had known were growing fast. Nancy missed the McKinney family. Robert was busy running their gristmill close by their home and Susie had her hands full taking care of the family. A few miles made a big difference in being able to visit.

Susan (Susie) Dale and Robert McKinney were a generation younger than Nancy and Bill Buchanan. Susie, a redhead, boasted that she was the belle of three counties when she married Robert in the late 1870's. Some of their children were married now and had their own home. Lafayette (Fate), Hickey, Tom, and Lester were youngsters and Nora was unmarried and still at home.

Fons was one of seven sons and had three sisters. Susan had ruled the ten children with a firm hand. According to family stories the seven boys would be lined up and Susan would give each a switching. One would say, "But I didn't do anything to be punished for today." She would say, "Well, you will by tomorrow."

"I believe they are already in the wagon." Fons nodded to Nancy. "Hattie, we'd best go. It's a long ride home. Good to see you, Mrs. Buchanan." He walked to Vance and shook his hand, nodded to Jane, and he and his family walked away from the family cemetery. (I don't know if Rachel is buried in the "McKinney Cemetery" across the Blue Ridge Parkway at McKinney Gap, at the cemetery close by Pepper's Creek or the cemetery where her father, Charles McKinney, is buried.)

◆

Riding in the wagon was rough going for Hattie. Sitting with a wide board at her back, she clutched her stomach thinking she could protect the baby from the jolting. A piercing pain cut through her back, and she couldn't hold back a groan. Looking up, she looked into Fons' eyes and then at Lawrence.

"You have two months to go, Hattie. It's not coming yet, surely." Raising his voice, Fons called to his pa to slow down and 'watch the ruts in the road.' Hattie lowered her head. "You can say that and I can hope that, but the baby can come anyway."

Much later, the wagon pulled up to the cabin that Hattie, Lawrence, and Fons, called home. Fons jumped out and lifted his arms for Lawrence. When Lawrence toddled close he swung him from the wagon to the ground. Hattie turned until she could grasp the back of the wagon and levered her body to an upright position. Robert jumped down and he and Fons helped Hattie step down to a rung in the wagon wheel and then to the ground.

"I believe I need to lie down, Fons. Maybe the babe will settle down." She murmured under her breath, 'Surely we can keep it there for two more months. Fons wants another son, please Lord.'

Susie asked, "Do you want me to stay, Hattie? Is it time?" When Hattie didn't reply, Susie and Robert looked at each other then he climbed into the wagon. Turning to Fons she called out. "You come for me, if the pain won't let up. Babies are born whether it's time or not."

Hattie clutched her protruding belly as she walked slowly toward the flat stones serving as steps up to the small stoop and the entrance to the cabin. Fons took Lawrence up with one arm and stepped up to Hattie. "Here, lean on me." He put his other arm around her waist as she stepped up to the stoop, and he opened the door to the dark, cool room.

She walked to a bed in the corner of the room, and lay on top of the covers. "I'll just rest a minute. I know you and Lawrence are hungry. Just a minute." He watched as her lids closed and a soft whistle sounded through her open lips. Asleep, he thought, turning away.

He walked to the open fireplace, lifting the lid from the bread skillet. Seeing flatbread left from the morning, he lifted it out and placed it on a plate sitting on the table. He turned to Lawrence, lifted him into his arms, and went out the door. "I'll get milk from the springhouse. A little apple-butter with the bread and we've got supper, huh, boy?"

Lawrence squirmed to get down but Fons held tight. "No. Stay with me. I don't know where the snakes are this time of day but they're around. I've killed more copperheads this summer than last. You'd think they would be scarce, huh?" He opened the door to the springhouse and waited for his eyes to focus in the dark, cool room. He looked carefully in each corner and crevice, before entering to lift the crock of milk out of the cold water. He backed out and fastened the door.

After supper Hattie wanted to sponge off. Fons brought water for the kettle, stoked up the fire, and watched as she found a bathing cloth and brought a chair close to the fire. She would tip the heated water into the pan that sat by the hearth.

"I need to milk old 'Bossy' and see to feeding the stock. I'll take Lawrence." Bending down he picked up his son. "I'll just take you out so you can relieve yourself. You're learning how to pee standing up, aren't you, boy? Pretty soon you'll be teaching your brother."

Hattie was quiet when they came back. She had changed into her sleeping gown and was standing in front of the pan. "I'll just put Lawrence to bed. Will you throw out the water, Fons?"

Walking to the hearth he leaned down and picked up the pan. With light from the fire the water in the pan looked rose colored. "You're bleeding!"

14

Grassy Creek, Mitchell County, N.C.

Jane and her family spent the night at her mother's house. With Lula and her daddy gone it seemed empty to her. Joe and Emily had a new baby, Texie Missouri, and little Maude helped fill the house. They gave Nancy a reason to keep going, but she saw her mother looking to Buchanan's Ridge and the cemetery, where her heart lay buried.

Jane and little Effie still slept in the attic room, but Vance slept on a pallet in front of the fire. It was difficult for him to climb the steps now.

Nancy took Jane's hand and they walked to the porch after supper. "You look tired, Jane, and you've lost weight, you and Vance both. Is he any better do you think?"

"No, Mother. I think he's losing ground. He can't hold out to do much so I spend a lot of time in the garden and taking care of the animals. Uncle Bob and Aunt Becky come by to help out. His brothers come, too." She signed and turned her head away. "They have things to do, too, so we try to put a good face on it. They know, though." A tear slipped down Jane's cheek.

"What does the doctor say?" Nancy reached and wiped her daughter's tears.

"He said something about wasting disease and told Vance to eat lots of red meat. He just seems to get weaker, though." Turning to her mother, she touched her hand. "Vance feels bad about what has happened and how it affects Effie and me. He tries hard but nothing seems to help."

Jane hitched her shoulders and signed deeply. Looking out at the surrounding mountains, she felt a peace, like they were a part of her. "Mother, I read the Bible at night after supper. I read about the trials of God's people, and think of the hurt you and Daddy had. How did they stand up to it? How do you?"

Nancy looked off into the distance. "Do you pray, Jane? You must pray for strength to bear the pain. You can't ask Him to deliver you from your trials, just to give you courage to go on. Pray, Jane, and if you're lucky, the gift of love, from your family and those you love, will see you through." Standing, Nancy walked to a bucket of water sitting on the top step. "Come, Jane. Let's walk to the cemetery. I planted a slip from the (Pee Gee) hydrangea Bill loved so, close by his grave. I water it each day while I tell him about my day."

That night, as Jane lay in the bed beside Effie, she thought of her mother's grief for her husband. Somehow tending the hydrangea at Bill's grave was giving her some ease. It's like my peace when I see the mountain peaks, she thought. Maybe looking at a mountain will give me strength and courage. I believe if I could be *lifted to the shoulders of a mountain*, I would be at home. When she prayed she asked for courage and strength in caring for her family.

The next day Nancy and Jane went to church alone. Jane thought how proud her Father had been of this new church he and his neighbors had built in 1900. They had just taken their seats when a friend came to them. "Come quick. Dock is hurt bad."

Before services a group of men had congregated outside that included Jane's brother, Dock Buchanan. Dock had a falling out with a neighbor over a stray hog. He had slaughtered the hog, saying it was his, while the other man said, no, it was his. Before anyone knew what was happening, they were fighting. Suddenly a knife flashed. Those close by kept Dock alive. His wife folded her cotton shawl and pressed it against the wound. Someone rushed into the church, removed the stovepipe from the wood burning stove, and dumped the soot directly on Dock's wound. It quickly clotted the bleeding. Nancy brought a doctor to help tend her son and he gradually was able to be up and about, but unable to lead his normal, robust life. This new tragedy would bear heavily in the years to come.

15

An End In Chestnut Grove

Hattie was in labor. She had spotted continuously the past month and knew the baby had to come soon or he wouldn't live. Her water broke while she was stirring the boiling clothes. She dragged herself up to the stoop, and rested until she could get up and go to the bed. She hoped Fons and Lawrence would come home from the fields soon.

Fons had lifted Lawrence onto the back of the horse pulling the plow. His little son had flung his arms around the horse's neck, and joyously talked the old horse forward. Holding to the plow, his daddy bent to the job.

Life was hard here. He had known nothing in his short life that caused him to think it should be different for him than it had been for his mam and pap. Mopping his face with a cotton square, he looked towards his house, wondering about Hattie.

He knew things weren't right with her. Would the baby live? He thought of his cousin who had recently died of the measles, along with her young child. She was buried with her child and her niece of 4 months.

Looking up at the sun, he turned the old horse and walked him to a large tree where a trough of water waited. "It's time to eat, boy. I'll just unhitch old Bob here and we'll walk him to the barn, after he's watered some. Just hang on when he lowers his head." Lawrence giggled then clutched his mane as old Bob ducked his head to drink.

Walking into the house, Fons saw Hattie sitting on the bed. She was trying to get out of her clothes that were wet and sticking to her legs. Lifting her head, she looked at him. She was pale and her eyes were shiny with fear. "Can you take Lawrence to your daddy and bring Susie back? My water broke while I was outside, so the baby has to come."

He walked to her and began to help her undress. This was new to him and his hands were clumsy. Turning to Lawrence, he said, "I'll get you a bite to eat, and then we'll go to Papa Robert's house. Get a clean shirt from the box under the bed; then go to the porch and wash your face and hands. You're a big boy now. Just don't go off the porch."

Turning back to Hattie, he helped her stand, and pushed her dress down so she could step out of it. Her drawers were wet and stained, so he stripped them off.

"There's some hot water in the kettle. Help me sponge off and I'll just get in the bed. Go to the trunk and get those old quilts so I won't ruin our bed. Oh, Fons, hurry back with Mama Susie. I'm going to need her."

Color was flooding Fons' face and neck as he bent to his wife and tried to clean her body of the bloody fluid. His mind was a blank but his body seemed to be able to follow instructions. He turned and lifted the lid from the trunk. He pulled several quilts from the depths and dumped them on the foot of the bed.

"Can you stand while I spread the quilts?" He put his arm beneath Hattie's and lifted her against him. He spread the quilts with the other hand and laid her gently on their bed.

Looking up he saw Lawrence standing where he had left him. His little face was pale as he stared at his mother. "Is Mama sick, Dada?" He settled onto the floor like a little puddle.

Fons picked up his little son and turned to Hattie. "Try to get some sleep. I'll be back before you know it."

"There's some cold biscuits on the table. Spread a little jam on them. That will do Lawrence until he gets to your Papa's." Her words were too late. They were already out the door.

◆

Fons walked away from the cabin and gristmill, not stopping or looking back until he topped the ridge and could look back from a safe distance. They still stood on the porch: his pap and mam, with Lawrence between them. He lifted his hand and walked away, leaving behind the grave holding Hattie, another his infant son, Wayne. He still heard little Lawrence calling for his Dada, and Mama.

He stopped and sank to the ground. Blue mountains shading to purple reached up, surrounding him. A soft breeze lifted the leaves from nearby trees, releasing the fresh, clean smell of sourwood blossoms. Grass bent and danced beside his face, soothing like the soft touch of a known hand.

He looked but didn't see; felt the grass tickle his face, but didn't notice, smelled the familiar aroma, but didn't know these familiar comforts. How did he get here?

At sixteen Hattie was so pretty. Flirting with her was an easy ritual. After all, they were young and life seemed an endless road. He still didn't know how it happened, but he had married and had a son. Now she was dead and another son lay buried.

Hattie had struggled for two days to give birth. When the tiny baby finally emerged from her body, he was as battered as his mother. The fact that they both lived seemed a miracle. Her mother-in-law, Susie, tended them both, and saw that Hattie's milk came on and the little boy was able to suckle.

Susie cleaned and cooked enough to leave them food for a while. Robert came for a visit and they all agreed that it was safe for her to go home for a few days. They left and came back several times for the next couple of weeks. Hattie was up and taking care of little Wayne and Lawrence, but she didn't look well. As Susie got ready to leave this time, she was worried.

She took Fons aside. "Hattie was torn when the baby came," she told him. "I've put salve on it but it doesn't look good. It's angry looking. I think she may have a fever and it's affected her milk. Little Wayne isn't getting enough. I think we'd better find a doctor. Robert and I will send Lester or Hickey when we get home. We'll take Lawrence with us."

The doctor came and found Fons trying to sooth his little infant son. Hattie had convulsed with fever in the night and stopped breathing. He lifted the baby from Fons' arms, and told him to get cows milk. They would try to get him to take some.

Fons walked to where Hattie lay and stared down at his wife. Her pretty hair had lost its luster. It was almost the same color as her pale face. Lifting his hand he brushed a strand away from her cheek. Turning away, he walked out the door.

In the weeks that followed Susie and her daughter, Nora, struggled to save the baby. If they had been able to find a wet nurse it may have made a difference, but he was weak from the time of his birth. They soon buried him at the foot of his mother's grave.

16

Tennessee

Fons got to his feet, looked for the trail, and began walking towards the road. Pushing his morbid thoughts away, he began thinking of his plans. He would walk through the day, sleep on the ground, and make the camp where the railroad was being built in a few days, near Johnson City. (This railroad was a forerunner of the Clinchfield that would come down through Alta Pass and on down to Marion in later years.)

He was taken on a team of workers without much trouble. His day started before dawn, stumbling towards coffee boiling over a fire. He waited his turn for a flat, unleavened pat of bread coming off the fry pan, unless it was his turn to cook.

He hauled wheelbarrow loads of debris from the blasting sites until his legs ached and his arms couldn't answer his demand to lift the barrow one more time.

Fons walked to his tent. Covered with dust and his throat parched, he fell onto his makeshift bed, too tired to care if he missed supper. Thank the Lord I don't have to cook tonight, he thought. Rolling over he was soon asleep, but woke in thirty minutes looking for food.

His crew took turns cooking. There was a firm rule that anyone who complained about the cooking lost his place in line, and had to cook the very next night. Fons had cooked several nights ago and looked forward to a stretch of other men's cooking. One of the men sitting back with his plate said, not thinking, "The cornbread's burned." He recovered in time to say, "But I like it that way."

Fons had been part of the railroad building crews for some months now. So far his group had stayed out of trouble. He had befriended two brothers who had worked for the crews for several years. They sat around the campfire at night talking about what they would do when they were close to a town. If all went well, it would be soon.

Their brother had been killed in an avalanche of rocks and dirt last year. Sometimes the engineers who set the dynamite could misjudge and more came down than they anticipated. Thinking about him tonight, the two brothers began talking about their earlier years. One day stood out in their mind.

"The day we decided to leave the foothills and start up the mountain turned out better than expected. We came through a place called Buck's Creek some miles from Marion. We heard tell that a good trail would take us up. We had slept rough in a grove of trees, overlooking a holding with a log house and barn. We'd seen a man tending to his chores, and watched as his lamplight blinked out. We'd decided to take his mules after we had slept a few hours. Boy, were we surprised to find the sun up, as he rode out on horseback with another leashed horse trailing behind. Course we crept up to the house, looking window to window. There was no one to home!"

Puzzled Fons waited to hear more. He suspected he had been cozying up to thieves and wondered what would come out next.

"Well, seeing there was no one at home, not even in the necessary, we took what we needed from the house, and with the two mules to ride, struck out for the trail." Billy smiled slyly. "O'course we took our time, not wanting to catch up, you know."

Fons yawned and stretched. "Well, I reckon we'll be getting to the mountains in Mitchell County before long. I look forward to that." He got up and strolled towards his tent.

Billy and John looked at each other. "Did you know he was from around there, John? I do believe we've talked out of turn, don't you?"

"Well, its too late now, Billy. Let's just hope he didn't hear the tale from another mouth. Sure wouldn't want to hurt Fons, would we?"

◆

What seemed a year later, the railroad crew walked into camp at Alta Pass in Mitchell County, North Carolina. They had money for a hot bath and Fons didn't begrudge a cent, as he slipped into a tub full of steaming water. The long months it had taken them to get here were the most grueling of their hard work. Cold creek baths to keep the critters at bay were a necessity, not something to look forward to. Washing your own clothes and eating men's cooking, all of these experiences washed away with the hot water. As he pulled on his worn clothes his thoughts turned to his family, to little Lawrence.

He had been sending money to his mam and pap as regular as he was able. After hearing Billy and John's tale of their thievery, he kept a close watch on his money and his own safety. He was careful to keep up the friendship, seeking them out for talk around the fire. Fons knew to keep them close. Better to see the front of them and not turn his back. He knew they wanted to stay around for the girls and maybe some cards. He planned to slip away as soon as they were occupied. He wanted to stop by his Uncle Tom McKinney's place and then go on to his pap's house.

The next night was dark. No moon and a little drizzle allowed his careful steps away from the camp to go unnoticed. He knew the trails and made good time. As the sky was lightening, Fons approached his uncle's place. He saw his Uncle Tom walking towards the house carrying a pail.

Walking forward he called out. "Howdy, Uncle Tom. Do you reckon Aunt Jane (Dale) could feed me? I haven't had a woman's cooking lately." Tom's face was grave as he set his pail down and stood looking at Fons. Then a smile crossed his face as he stepped forward and gave Fons a big hug. "Son, you're a sight for sore eyes. Jane and I have thought a lot about you since all your troubles." Looking closely at him, he said, "Are you all right, then?"

Fons ran his hands over his face, looking down at the ground, then up at his uncle. He cleared his throat. "Well, thank you for your kindness. I reckon I don't know. I've spent my days working hard enough so I don't remember my dreams at night. I'll come to terms with it now, I guess."

Tom took Fons by the arm, picking up a pail of eggs as he walked them to the kitchen door. Jane turned from the stove. "Laws a mercy, it's Fons. Come in and sit. I've got creamed corn and fried chicken for breakfast. Old Tom here wanted something special this morning. Guess he knew who was coming." She moved both men to her table and began bringing the food.

When she took biscuits from the oven, Fons could feel tears coming. Brushing them away he asked if he could say a prayer of thanksgiving. Watching them bow their heads, he closed his eyes and prayed. Murmuring "Amen" he truly felt a lifting of his burdens.

17

Crossroads
In Mitchell County, 1905

Fons was walking towards the road through Grassy Creek. He had left Uncle Tom and Aunt Jane soon after breakfast, being anxious to see about his family. Following a worn path through the laurels, which would connect to the road towards home, he heard a gurgle of water. Hoping to have a cool drink, he parted a patch of large fern, looking for a spring. He saw a female form bending over a little branch. She was dipping the hem of her petticoat into the water and wiping her face. He must have made a sound because she turned with a look of alarm, her face showing streaks of red, and tears brimming from her eyes.

Fons stepped back, holding up his hands to show he meant her no harm. She stood and without taking her eyes from him, moved a few more steps away. "Are you hurt Misses? Can I help?" Fons stood his ground and kept his hands at his side. "My name is Fons McKinney. I left my Uncle Tom McKinney's place earlier and I'm on my way to see my pap, Robert McKinney."

"I'm Hester. Hester Stafford." Darting quick glances around her, with her hands gripped together, she tried a stiff little smile. "I heard the sound of this here spring and thought to wash up a bit." Her shoulders relaxed as she took a deep breath. Fons caught his breath when he was able to focus on her as she turned. She was a beauty!

His brain began to work as he spoke. "Can I take you to your husband, Misses?"

"Well, I'm not married, Mr. McKinney. Are you? Married, I mean."

Fons just looked at her. "Can I take you safely home then?"

They both turned as a voice said, "Looks like her pappy's here to do that, right Hestie?" Fons looked to Hester and watched as her face fell. He looked up at a large man who shifted his feet, folded his arms, and looked directly at him.

"Mr. Stafford?" The man nodded. "I'm Fons McKinney from around Chestnut Grove. Do you know it? My pap runs a grist mill close by."

Nodding, Stafford leaned over and picked a stalk of grass. Putting it in his mouth, he worried it around. "Well, you didn't answer my girl. Are you married Mr. McKinney?"

Fons looked directly into his eyes, man to man. "I was married, Mr. Stafford. My wife died, leaving behind a baby boy who followed her in death. I have a living son who is four years old. I reckon I need to get on. I'll be bidding you good day. Hester." He turned to her and then began to walk away.

"Well, hold on now. It's nigh on noon and we have some vittles in the wagon. It's just off the road over yonder. Hestie and me brought a load of 'tators and such from over near Estatoe. We've managed to sell all we brought so we'll be heading home right soon."

"I'd best get on home. I have a little grub and it's a long walk." Smiling and nodding at the two he turned and started down the path.

"Well, if you are in our territory any time soon, just drop by. Hester here would be glad to see you. She's a right smart girl and would make a man a good wife, I believe. Just about everybody around Estatoe can point you in the right direction." Fons swung around and found both of them looking at him.

"It's good meeting the two of you." Puzzled but smiling a little, he walked away. Pondering Hester's reddened face and what looked like tears, he wondered what had caused her upset. If it was her pap, what could he have done? He tried to put them out of mind and hurried toward his own responsibilities.

◆

Fons heard the creaking of the water wheel as he approached the home place. With the corn dried, Robert's neighbors would be bringing some to be ground into cornmeal.

Looking around he saw chickens scratching in the yard and saw the mica sparkling in the sun. An old yellow cat was lying in the shade of the barn. Looking up at the house he saw his mam with her arms folded, just standing on the porch looking at him. Taking his hat off, he walked towards her. Climbing the steps, he stood in front of her waiting for her words or movement. She didn't disappoint.

"Well, Fons." She lifted her hands to the scarf covering her head, patting it to make sure it was in place, then lifted her arms and held both of his. "Are you home for good or will you go back to railroading."

"I'm here now, Mam, so the rest will come in good time. Where's Lawrence?"

She looked at him with a stern face. "As you can see, I'm well. If you want to know, your pa, Nora, and your brothers are well. Lawrence is a strong boy and he doesn't miss a chance to get his own way. He probably won't remember the pa that left him." With that punch, she dropped her hold on his arms and stepped back.

He looked beyond her and saw his sister, Nora, standing in the open doorway and a young lad with his arms wrapped around her legs. Nodding to Nora, he walked around his mam and stooped down in front of Lawrence. "Boy, I'm your pap. It's time we get to know each other."

His son spent some time looking him over, than his eyes settled on his face. "I don't even look like you. How are you my pap?"

"Been looking in your mama's mirror, have you? Well, I'm your pap. You have your mama's looks but you are my son." Taking his arm, Fons pulled Lawrence to his side. "Now let's go see your grandpap. I thought you would be helping him by now. You're big enough."

"Nora says I don't need to work. Someone sends money to take care of me."

"That's me, son, and I work hard for that money. It's time you learn that true fact." And with that retort, he pulled the boy along as he walked toward the mill. Coming through the door, he saw his pap lifting a sack of ground corn atop another by the door. As Robert lifted his head his eyes locked on Fons.

"Son! The Lord be praised." Walking close, he pulled Fons to his chest. There were tears in both their eyes, but their smiles made a mockery of them. Lawrence looked back and forth between them, not satisfied that he knew what was happening. Robert glanced down and said, "Lawrence, this is your pa and my son. You'll be proud of that, as I am. Yes, siree, you will."

Fons walked the home place with his pap, taking in what work needed doing. The first morning, he got Lawrence out of bed as he got up. They took breakfast and headed out as the sky began to lighten. Lawrence's complaining became crying and then a full-blown conniption fit. His dad put him over his knee and gave him three sharp slaps on his rear. Lawrence was so shocked his mouth fell open without a cry or word coming out. "Now son, I expect you to do what I ask without protest. That is the first duty you must learn. My word is your law. Do you understand?" "But, Nora," he started.

Fons took his arms and looked him in the eye. "Nora is your aunt. She took the place of your mam for the past year and I thank her for it, but you've always been my son and what I say goes. Now, you and I need to help clean the inside of the mill. I'll show you what to do." Fons sure hoped that Nora would give up her charge without too much trouble, because he intended to take a wife, one that would be a comfort to him and a mother to his boy. When and how he would do this were questions he couldn't answer now.

At supper he listened as his family related who had done what to someone they knew.

Susan started the news. "You remember Dock Buchanan and his knife wound? It may have passed you by since it happened around the time of your loss. Well, he's still poorly but Dovie gave birth to another boy this year, so he must be right pert some of the time. That family has seen a lot of trouble. Jane's husband, Vance Snipes, is bad sick, I hear. Brights Disease. No cure you know."

Nora took up the tale. "You remember Nancy's youngest son, Joe, and his wife, Emily? They live with her. Well, Emily is expecting another baby, too. They lost their first child, a daughter they named Texie Missouri, in the year you lost Hattie and Wayne. Now Nancy has two of Bud's children with her. With all her troubles, she seems happier with young ones at her house again." (Texie Missouri Buchanan is buried at Buchanan's Cemetery, close by her dad, Joe Neal Buchanan.)

Robert spoke up. "You know how news travels around here. This piece hain't none of our business or anyone else's, I reckon, but it's being told. Nancy (Buchanan) inherited one eighth of the 150 acres down on the waters of Pepper's Creek, owned by her mother, Rachel. She's sold it to J. A. McBee." (McDowell County, Deed book 36, page 179)

Fons looks up from his plate. "I'd be surprised if Nancy or some of Jane's family don't see to her pretty regular. Do Jane and Vance have more children? I reckon they are still down around Buck's Creek?"

"They're still there." His pa took up the conversation. "Vance has family to help out and that makes it easier on Jane, Nancy tells us." Looking at Fons, he kind of murmurs, "Effie is it for them, and it's probably for the best."

18

Mitchell County, 1906

Fons walked to his cabin, about too tired to get up the steps. He started to get a dipper of water from the bucket hanging by the door, but it was empty. He walked through the open door expecting to see Hester getting some food together. The room was empty. Slowly turning, he looked at the unmade beds, then the unwashed dishes on the table. No fire, just gray ashes in the fireplace.

He sat on the unmade marriage bed, and put his face in his hands. Hearing the jingle of harness and a gruff voice talking to someone, he got up and walked out the door. His pap and Lawrence were sliding off the back of a horse. "Papa, Papa. I stayed with Pap all day. What do you think about that?"

"Well, son, that's fine. How did you get there?" Fons walked to meet them.

"That Hester and one of her friends took me by. He had a wagon and they took her clothes and all. She must be going somewhere."

"I guess so, son. Ya'll come in while I start up the fire. I sure am hungry. How about you?" Robert and Lawrence followed him into the house. Fons bent over and scooped the dead ashes aside. He felt some good grace when he saw there was kindling and wood and soon had a fire going.

Robert McKinney sat in a chair by the fire and stared at his son. "How is the work going on the road?"

"It's mostly grubbing out the stumps now. Hard on man and beast but worth it, I reckon. Pay is poor though. Looks like I can't make much headway." He put his head back in his hands. Looking up he said, "I believe it's time to end this marriage with Hester, Pap. I made a mistake and that's a fact."

"What'll you do?"

"I'll go to Bakersville (county seat of Mitchell County) and start legal proceedings in the court. I know it'll kill Mam, but I don't have a choice that I can see. I'll see to it right away. Maybe I'll feel some peace in my heart when it's done."

With that he walked out the door, took the pail from the porch and headed for the spring. He came back, hung the full bucket by the door, and was carrying milk from the springhouse. Pouring some cornmeal and milk in a pot, he swung it over the fire. "We can eat some mush and maybe I can think straight if I get something in my belly."

19

McDowell County, 1908

Effie was crying again. "I don't want to go to school, Mama. Do I have to go?" Jane put the button through the last loop on Effie's coat, patting her shoulder as she rose to her feet. "Yes, you must go. Remember, your daddy wants you to go." Jane reached over and wiped Effie's face, pulling her into a hug. "But I don't want to leave him today. He didn't kiss me goodbye and won't say anything." Jane leaned to kiss her daughter's cheek. "He's just tired because he didn't sleep well. I'm going to give him a good bath and then he'll feel like taking a little broth. I expect he'll sleep most of the day and when you get home, he'll be right ready to see you. Hurry now, your cousins will be waiting for you. It's still cold in April." She watched as Effie shuffled out the door.

Jane watched her walk to the little group of children then closed the door. She moved to the rocking chair in front of the fireplace and sat, her shoulders slumping. Not sleeping more than a few hours each night in months was draining her strength. She knew she should ask Vance's family to help her tend him. Maybe some of the older children could take turns. Standing, she walked into the kitchen to the stove, where water was simmering in the kettle. She carried it to the bedroom to pour in the bathing pan sitting beside Vance's bed.

Stacked cloths were on a chair for bathing and drying his shriveled body. The room was fairly warm with heat coming through the door. She had kept him in their bedroom so Effie wouldn't see him in his worse moments. Jane slept on a cot next to his bed so she could hear him in the night. She remembered her time with Lula when she tended her those years back. *I guess the good Lord knew what was ahead. He prepared me.*

Jane smoothed her reddened hand over his forehead and brushed his lank hair back from his face. She was afraid to wet his head to wash his hair, for fear of pneumonia. Maybe when the weather warmed up she could do it. As she looked at his face, Vance opened his eyes. His eyes searched her face, and relaxed as he felt her hand's caress.

◆

Bob and Becky Buchanan came by the next day. They looked into Jane's tired eyes. "Oh Jane, you are exhausted. Come sit down with us. We need to make plans to get you help."

Jane couldn't stop the tears from forming in her eyes. Their sympathetic expression took away her bravery. "I do need help, but everyone does so much, helping with the animals and garden. Goodness, you killed our hogs and worked all the meat. You all have so much to do yourself. I was thinking that I could ask some of Vance's nephews to take turns sitting with him, and maybe I can relax enough to sleep some. Effie is becoming more aware too and she's frightened."

"Well, we can't have you getting sick. You need some rest." Becky reached over and took her hand. "Effie is what, nine years old? I know it's hard but she'll need to know that her daddy won't get well. Do you let her help feed him? I think you need to give her more responsibility, to help you out some."

Jane nodded her head. "I haven't taken the time to teach her what she needs to know about housekeeping while I've been so busy with Vance. You're right, Becky, I need regular help. I could hire a girl. Do you know of someone? Could you tell the family? Maybe they know someone who needs the work."

Bob and Becky agreed to ask about and had suggestions about who could come now to help out. Jane felt some of her burdens lifted just knowing they were there to help. Eventually they started exchanging news.

Jane told them of Joe and Emily's little girl, Carrie, who was born in March of this year, and about little Mamie, who was three years old now. "Joe is working on the railroad, helping to build a trestle across a deep pass, down near Bostic Junction (McDowell County). Dock and Dovie have had another boy. I declare Mother is worried about that family."

Bob said he had run into Robert McKinney, down at Marion, a few weeks back. "It seems Fons remarried several years ago, a woman from Estatoe. Hester Stafford is her name. According to Robert she's quite a beauty, but he had a sad expression on his face while telling the story. I didn't say much, just stood companionable like. He shuffled his feet some and made the remark that 'She didn't take to being a mother.' I believe there's a story there but I didn't ask questions. He asked about you, Jane, and said his family sends their regards."

Jane felt a shiver when she heard Fons' name. She didn't have a name for how he affected her. She tried to smile but felt it probably didn't pass muster. Bob and Becky didn't seem to notice, though.

They heard a commotion outside. Before they could get up, the door burst open and Jane's brother, John Henry, came striding into the room. As Jane stood up he swept her into his arms. "How's my girl?" He tilted her chin and looked into her eyes. "Well, I've brought Mother and she'll see you right, I reckon. We've been awful worried, Jane. You haven't written for some weeks."

Jane looked at the door as her mother came in with a satchel. Seeing Bob and Becky, she gave a big smile. "We hoped to see you two. Bob, you look more like Bill everyday and I thank you for a glimpse of his face. John Henry, see to the horse and wagon. I'll just rest my weary bones and then we can take supper. Jane, you need some rest. Go lie down for a while and John and I'll check on Vance. Becky, I brought food already cooked so I hope you and Bob will eat with us." With that, she drew a deep breath and sat.

Becky looked at Jane and smiled. "Come with me, Jane. I'm going to fill a tub for you and help scrub your back. You can take a long nap and we'll see to things." She walked towards the kitchen.

Jane looked from one kind face to another. Her loved ones were here. She turned and followed her aunt from the room.

◆

Rested, Jane sat beside Vance's bed. He had fresh clothes and had taken some broth. His pillows were pulled up and fluffed so he could sit up. Effie was curled up beside him on the bed while Nancy and John Henry were in chairs around his bed.

Taking Vance's hand, Jane spoke up. "Mother, tell us about Joe and Emily's little Carrie. Will they be all right without you to help out?"

John Henry laughed, slapping his leg. "Well, I'll bet they are doing fine. Maude and Freddie (Bud and Sally Ann's children) are visiting their Elliott kin. That gives Joe and Emily a chance to be alone with their little family. Just like Emma Jane loves to have a little time when I'm not underfoot. Yep, it all works out."

Vance laughed, kind of a croak like. Jane squeezed his hand lightly because she knew how sensitive his skin was now. He looked down at Effie who had fallen asleep and a tear escaped his eye. He looked up at Jane. This little family togetherness would be soon gone. His eyes conveyed this knowledge.

Nancy sighed. "Carrie is a beauty just like Mamie. Emily is strong and is doing well. She misses Joe awful the times he's gone. When we get back he'll be going back to work on the trestle. Have mercy! From what he tells us it's going up from the ground and it's going high. I worry, but try not to let on. Emily needs to keep her milk up for the baby, and worrying about Joe won't help that."

"Mother, how is Dock? I know Dovie just gave him another son, but I hear he's mighty poorly."

"Well, Jane, he sure hain't well. I can tell by looking that he's got some kind of sickness. I believe he has night sweats. I'm afraid he's sick inside from that knife cut. Whatever, it don't keep him from his husbandly duties!"

Jane sees that Vance is asleep. She leans over and slips the pillows down and lifts his frail body to a reclining position. John Henry had risen to help but saw that Jane had the routine well in hand. She spoke quietly. "John, carry Effie to her bed and I'll be right in to see to you and Mother." Leaning over him she stroked Vance's hair back, then tucked the covers around his body. Looking at her husband, perhaps she saw the moments of opportunity they had missed.

◆

John Henry and Nancy stayed for several days, and Jane was able to get some rest. That and having her family with her made all the difference. She began to get some light in her eyes and her face relaxed. Effie saw the difference, too.

"Mama, you look younger today. How does that happen?" Jane laughed. "Well, it's because I see you and Mother smile, and I hear John Henry working around the place, singing a tune. I do believe your Daddy feels better, too. Did you notice?" "No Mama, I don't believe he feels better. I believe he's too tired to feel better."

"Effie, will you come and sit by me. I need to talk about Daddy." Jane walked to Effie, sat in the rocking chair, and pulled her into her lap. Lifting her chin she looked into her eyes. "Effie, it's true Daddy won't get well. He is too sick and, yes, too tired, but remember this. The Lord is watching over him like we are and when he gets too tired, He will come and take him to Heaven."

Jane saw the terror in Effie's eyes and the screams building in her throat. She lifted her and walked out the door. She didn't stop until they were in the thick of the trees. Jane held her tight while whispering in her ear. "Don't, until we are far enough from the house. We don't want your daddy to hear. He'll know, Effie, he'll know and he wants to keep this true fact from you." Finally, Jane sat on a rock and cradled her little nine-year-old. "Now, cry baby. Cry all you want."

Effie did cry and couldn't be consoled. Nancy and John Henry helped her by their presence, as did Vance's family after they left. Vance became unconscious and couldn't see his daughter's distress. He died on May 31, 1908. Jane was a widow and Effie was without a father.

After the funeral at Pleasant Gardens Baptist Church, Jane packed what she wanted to take, and locked the door of her home for the past ten years. She said goodbye to Uncle Bob and Aunt Becky, and to the Snipes family. Fond farewells were given amongst "We'll see you soon," and her brother was there again to take Effie and Jane to the house below Buchanan's Ridge. Jane was back to where she had started, close by her beloved mountains.

Book III

20

The Old House In Grassy Creek, 1908

Jane walked down the sloped land towards the creek below her mother's house. The leaves were drifting from the trees, sometimes going quite a distance, before settling softly up against an old stump or in the creek. She stopped at its edge and looked across at the two-story log house, where Robert and Susie McKinney had raised their family. It's possible, maybe before that time Susie had grown up there, too. It had been standing empty since Robert and Susie had moved away.

This house had become a part of her waking life and was often in her dreams. Asleep, she would wander through the rooms that had little alcoves and secret doors. In her dreams she would open the doors, and come face-to-face with the people of her life. She never saw any of the McKinney family in these dreams.

Today was different. She lifted her skirts and took steps on the rocks that allowed her to cross the creek. Taking a deep breath, she turned to look up the knoll to Nancy's house. She saw her mother on the porch, sitting in her favorite chair. Jane knew she was watching.

Turning her back, she faced the old house. The weeds growing around the house had seen several frosts. There were steps strong enough to take her to the porch. A door stood ajar. Jane closed her eyes for only a moment. She marched through the brush, pushing aside any that would impede her progress to the steps. She was up and pushing the door open before her next thought. The afternoon sun showed an empty room and narrow stairs leading up. There were no alcoves or secret doors. There would be. Her life here would create them.

◆

Effie was beginning to accept her father's death. Even in a house that seemed full of people, she had her mother to herself. Sleeping with her was the prize she collected everyday. She loved to help tend her little cousins, Carrie, and Mamie. Maude and Freddie didn't mind Effie taking some of their duties, and Effie was young enough to think this was in her favor.

With Joe away, Emily, Nancy, and Jane, made themselves busy keeping up the farm and doing the household duties. Still Jane felt the need to set up her own household. Joe was the man of the house. She wanted to give him and Emily their chance to be on their own, although Nancy and the children would still be there. Maude and Freddie, Bud and Sally Ann's daughters, planned to live with their brother, Wallace, for a while. The house down the hill seemed the answer. Did Robert McKinney's brother-in-law, G. R. Dale, still own the house? She would make inquiries at church.

Jane had sold her livestock down in Buck's Creek. She had turned her farm into a sharecropper type arrangement. A relative of Vance had set up his household there while paying Jane part of the sale of his crops as rent. With this income and some that Vance had put aside, she and Effie would be all right. Maybe she could rent the house down the hill.

◆

Nancy and Jane were trudging up Buchanan's Ridge. Nancy liked to see the graves covered with colored leaves, their coverlet for the winter. She liked to see the snow come early, adding another layer. This was her comfort, not for those lying under this hallowed ground. Jane could see her father smiling fondly at his wife's need to tend him even now.

They both stood with arms folded, gazing into their memories of these loved ones. Nancy spoke first. "I see you are thinking of setting up house across the creek. It's a big house for two people. Reckon Rufus Dale would rent it to you?"

Jane laughed. "Well, I should have known you would know my mind. Even though you sure didn't when you promised me to Vance Snipes." She turned to Nancy. "Mother, you know I had a grudge in my heart for some years, even before I struggled to take care of Vance. I wanted to forgive you but came to realize there was nothing to forgive. In the end it was my decision to ride off with him, even though I thought different then."

"You are a strong woman, Jane. You and your daddy didn't know it back there but I did. I'll talk to Rufus when I see him at church. Maybe if you fix up that house he'll give you a fair rent. Maude and I will help. You have enough furnishings to start out. Now tell me, what are your plans?"

"I plan to set up a life that will work for Effie and me. I won't be looking for a husband, Mother. One was enough. Yes, I'm strong and now I believe in myself. I may serve meals for the road crew. What do you think of that?"

Nancy's brown eyes gleamed. "I think, once we talk with Rufus, we better start planting the raspberry shoots near your garden spot. We'll need to hitch up the mule and turn your soil for your kitchen garden, so it'll be ready to work in the spring. We'll clear away the brush from around those old apple trees out back yonder and in the yard. The frost's done most of our work already. Lord, I wonder if John Henry or Molt has time to see to the outhouse. It sure needs attention."

"Well, let's go and see about the children." With that command she started down the slope, but stopped abruptly. She walked back to William's grave and stood for several minutes. Turning towards Jane, she took her hand. "I told him you're going to be all right now, Jane. I wanted him to know."

◆

November came in with high winds blowing snow. Nancy's sheep were huddled next to the barn, their thick wool keeping out the cold wind, when Effie came by with Maude from school. Effie blew on her hands when she removed her mittens before the fire. Maude helped her remove her coat. She shucked out of her own and hung both on a chair to dry out. "I just wonder how those sheep grow their wool so fast. Why, Mother Buchanan shears them down to their skin in the early summer. Have you noticed that, Effie?"

"I did. At first I hid my face, afraid I'd see them bleed. But, do you know what? She didn't nick a one. Not one. I believe she can do anything, don't you?"

"Well, she plans on teaching you to spin the wool into thread one of these first days. You notice that I can comb the burrs right out on that card. You could do that right now."

"I'm learning to clean out the cobwebs and such in the house. I declare these rooms get all kinds of critters during the summer. Remember when you and Grandma went to visit Uncle Dock, and Aunt Sis (Emily) took the children to visit her folks? Mama wouldn't let me in the house until she had checked each nook and cranny for snakes. Even then they could be hiding on a rafter or under the house, maybe. I think they're scary, Maude."

Laughing, Maude looked at Effie. "Your Mama pulled a trick on them snakes, Effie. She cleaned out the chimney, made a nice blaze in the fireplace, and put on a good backlog so it would burn for some time. She told Mother Buchanan all about it. Your mama was drawing the snakes to the warm. It worked, too. John Henry is the one who went in. With a sharp hoe, he did. I won't tell you that he didn't find one, because he found two. He made short work of those snakes so you don't have to worry, Effie. They were tricked and now they're dead. Mother Buchanan wasn't too happy since they were black snakes. They eat mice, you know."

◆

Jane hadn't heard from Rufus Dale, but noticed someone down at the McKinney place. The man was cutting and clearing out the brush around the orchard and house. She didn't go down but watched as he worked. He moved the leaning outhouse and put in new boards and seats before moving it back in place. Jane was sure someone was planning to occupy the house. Her shoulders slumped. It looked like her plans would have to wait.

Nancy met her on the porch. Frowning, she lifted her face to Jane. "I spoke to Rufus. He says you can move in his house without paying rent. I don't like it, Jane. People don't have a place fixed up and tell someone they can move in without paying rent. I smell a rat!"

"Someone is down there now. Do you know who it is?" Jane was trying to keep track of the man moving around the yard.

Nancy had her suspicions but shook her head, no.

21

Courtship

The family went to church together when Joe came home. Chestnut Grove Baptist Church welcomed him and Jane back to the congregation. Joe was a fine singer as was Jane. They still remembered how Bill Buchanan used to lead the singing and his strong voice. It seems Joe and Jane had his talent, too. Joe stood and sang a requested song.

1. *There's a home far away where no darkness ever came and I have many loved ones over there. I have spoken for a place and they are fixing me a room in that mansion bright and fair.*

2. *I have some precious friends whom I fear will wait too long. Till the day of his mercy will be past. Then how sad, oh how sad, for their chances all are gone. They'll be crying lost at last.*

3. *When you knock at the door and you cannot enter in, how you'll wish you had lived as Christian true. Then you'll think of what I say and the awfulness of sin will be waiting for you there.*

    Chorus: There'll be waiting, waiting, waiting for you. There'll be waiting, waiting, waiting for you.

(The words for this song were given to Effie Snipes McKinney, niece of Joe Buchanan, by Etta Mace, with the following message, dated August 15, 1971: "This song was in our Song Book in the year 1908 and is the last song that I ever heard Joe Buchanan sing.")

◆

Joe's visit was coming to an end. He was sitting in a rocker by the fire with little Carrie snuggled in his arms. A handsome man, he was tall and lanky with a nice mustache that curved down his mouth. "Since the weather has turned warm

91

again, I'll have to go back to Bostic Junction (Rutherford County, N.C.). I sure hope to be back home by Christmas."

Emily ducked her head, blinking back tears. She and Joe were a couple and she didn't do well when he was gone working for the railroad.

Nancy spoke up. "You write as soon as you get there. Me and Emily want to know where you are in case we need to get word." She laughed, looking over to Emily trying to get her to smile. It worked. "It sure is nice to have Jane and Effie close. I like to have my children where I can lay my hands on them." Murmuring under her breath, she said, "The numbers keep dwindling, my children."

◆

Jane was out on the porch getting wood for the cook stove. Looking up she saw a lone man starting up the slope to the yard. He raised his head and looked her in the eye as he removed his hat. It was Fons McKinney.

"I stopped by to pay my respects." He came up the steps and stopped before her. "How are you Jane? I'm sorry for your loss. I didn't get to know Vance but believe he was a good man."

Jane was so surprised to see Fons, she couldn't think. Effie was before the fire doing her lessons and Mamie and Carrie were napping. She needed to get back inside. "Thank you, Fons. The children are inside. Won't you come in and warm up. I don't think you've seen Effie since Granny Rachel's funeral."

He walked to the wood stack and loaded his arms. "Well, I'll make myself useful and I'd welcome seeing Effie again." He leaned past Jane and pushed open the door for her to enter. Following, he pushed it closed with his foot.

Effie glanced up, first looking at Fons and then her mother. "Who are you?"

"Hello, Effie. My name is Fons McKinney. I knew you, and your mama and dad, back when you were pretty young. I believe you met my son, Lawrence, at your great-granny's funeral. Do you remember?"

"Maybe," she said. "Where is Lawrence then, and his mama? My Granny and Aunt Sis aren't here, and Mama won't take visits from no man. Isn't that right, Mama?"

Jane's face reddened but she was able to laugh a little as she patted the top of Effie's head. "Fons and his family are friends of our family, Effie. Remember your manners. Did you look in to see if Carrie and Mamie are still asleep?"

Effie said, "How do." She lowered her head, then looked up at Jane. She nodded her head, yes. She had checked on the children.

"Have a seat, Fons, and tell me about Susie and Robert. I've seen Lester and Nora with Lawrence at church, but haven't seen your parents. I hope they aren't poorly. I wanted to speak with Nora and Lawrence, but they always got away. You know how it is with all the mingling and such."

"Mam and Pap have been troubled with sickness but are better now. Jane, I mainly came here to tell you about my situation. I've known you were back with Mrs. Buchanan for some time, and wanted to see you, but I tried to wait a decent time for your mourning your husband." He looked over at Effie who was frowning at him. "I wonder if you've heard that I married after Hattie's death?"

"Yes. Uncle Bob Buchanan saw your dad down in Marion. He said you had remarried several years ago. I hope you are all doing well." Effie had moved closer to her mama's rocker and laid her head against Jane's knees. She could feel her relax at Fons' words.

Fons bent forward and clasped his hands together. He had fine looking hands, Jane thought. He raised his head and looked directly at her. "My wife's name was Hester Stafford. Our marriage didn't work out. She left over a year ago and we are divorced. I wanted you to know that true fact from me."

"What's divorced, Mama?" Jane was dazed and didn't answer Effie. She just looked at Fons. Effie tugged on her skirt. "Mama?" They all turned their heads toward the door as it opened and Emily, Maude and Nancy, stepped in. They were bundled up with large wool scarves over their heads and coats.

"I just had word from Joe." Nancy handed a postcard to Jane. "You'll want to read it. He is such a cut-up."

Jane took the card and noticed the picture on the front. "Why, that's Joe amongst all those other men. He is right in front, like he was the focus of the picture." She turned it over and laughed as she scanned the words. "Listen to what he says Effie. At the top, written kind of in a curve, he says, *do you know who this is?* Then he has written the date. *Dec 6. 1908—Dear Mama, I am well at this time hope this will come safe and find you all well. Joseph Buchanan.*" She handed it to Effie. "You read it now. It's good practice."

Effie looked at the writing on the card: *Mrs. Nancy Buchanan, Mica NC Box No 3.* "It was sent Dec 7, 10 am with a one-cent stamp. Am I right?"

"You are." Jane pulled her up and gave her a hug. "You are a smart girl."

"I'm pleased he has arrived safe. Is everything all right with you, Jane?" Turning to Fons, she said, "I'm sorry about your troubles and glad you could come by." Emily left the room to check on her children.

Fons came to his feet, nodded at Nancy and Jane, and turned to go. Turning back, he said, "Jane it was good to see you and Effie. Hope to see you again soon, maybe at church." With that he opened the door and stepped outside.

Jane turned to Effie. "That was nice of Fons to come by. I'll see if I can help Emily get Carrie and Mamie up from their naps. Go on into the kitchen. Supper is warm and we'll just fill our plates. Mmmm. Fried apples, fresh tenderloin, with cornbread and milk. Effie, lift the window and get the pail of milk from the corner there. It may have ice on top but we can take care of that." Jane was talking to cover her thoughts. Fons divorced? Why hadn't she heard? What did he mean by wanting to tell her about it?

Effie had the covered pail on the table in a few minutes. Opening and closing the window brought in the cold air. Lifting the lid, she was able to pour around the ice into the waiting mugs. Looking up, she saw her mother through the door. "I don't like him."

Jane walked into the kitchen with Emily. "Who don't you like, Effie?"

"That man. Fons McKinney. I can tell, Mama. He came to call on you. He doesn't have a wife like we thought. I don't like him."

Jane was opening her mouth to reply when the door burst open. Fons and a strange man came into the room. His face was red and tears were streaming down his cheeks. He walked to Nancy and Emily. "Mrs. Buchanan." He looked from one to the other. "I've ridden all day to bring you news. It's bad news." Stepping back a step, he lowered his head then lifted his face to them again. "Joe's dead. He fell from the high trestle. I'm so sorry, but he's gone."

The author believes this is Joe Buchanan, brother of Melissa B. Schism, John Henry Buchanan, and Jane B. Snipes McKinney. Photograph belonged to Nancy Buchanan.

Postcard sent to Nancy D. Buchanan by her son Joe Buchanan, dated
December 6, 1908. The photo shows Joe and several of
his co-workers at Bostic Junction, N.C.

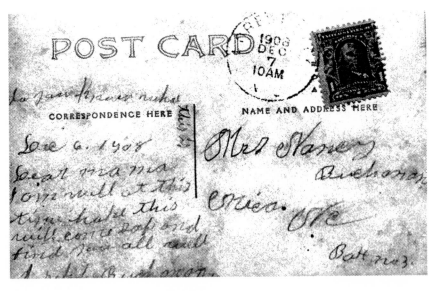

Message on postcard.

Gate at Buchanan Cemetery at the Switzerland Inn, Little Switzerland,
N.C. Photographs on this page are by Judy Carson.

Nancy D. Buchanan's Monument placed in cemetery by committee headed
by Judge Heriot Clarkson, Fons McKinney and George W. Butler
(second husband of Emily H. Buchanan Butler).

The following pages are photographs of Grave Markers in Buchanan Cemetery. Photographs are by Judy Carson.

Sarah Hollifield, sister of Elizabeth H. Buchanan.

Elizabeth Hollifield Buchanan, wife of Joseph H. Buchanan (parents of Robert, William A., Alford, George Buchanan and others).

Lula E. Buchanan, daughter of Nancy and William A. Buchanan.

Nancy and William A. Buchanan, parents of Melissa B. (Schism), Alford (Bud), James, William, John Henry, Daniel (Dock), Jane (Snipes McKinney), Joe, and Lula.

Texie Missouri Buchanan, daughter of Joe and
Emily Hollifield Buchanan.

Joseph Neal Buchanan, father of Texie, Carrie, and Mamie, son of Nancy
and William A. Buchanan.

Dovie, Carl, Daniel L. (Dock) Buchanan, daughter-in-law, grandson and son of Nancy and William A. Buchanan.

Pencil drawing of Nancy Deweese Buchanan by Frank Stanley Herring, ca 1930.

Oil on canvas of the Buchanan Cemetery by Sandra Gates of Charlotte and Burnsville, N.C., signed and dated 2005. (Gift by the artist to the author)

Susan, Nora and Robert P. McKinney (parents and sister of Fons McKinney and his siblings.)

22

Tragedy

Effie remembered being at Nancy's house when the family learned about Joe's death. She recalled how Nancy fell to her knees, grieving for her son.

Joe had fallen from the railroad trestle the crew was building down in Bostic Junction, early yesterday, December 16th. His friend had ridden all day to get here to tell his wife and mother. They were both in shock. Jane told Effie and Maude it would be necessary for them to help care for Carrie and Mamie. Jane would need to help Nancy and Emily through their grief. They both nodded, in awe of the circumstances.

Nancy was on her knees rocking her body back and forth, making a keening sound. Emily was sitting on the bed holding Carrie. Mamie was standing by the bed, eyes wide with fright. Jane sent Effie and Maude to Mamie. "See that she gets supper. Find a book and read to her." She bent to her mother and held her tightly in her arms. Nancy looked at Jane. "Bill and I made all the plans. All was taken care of, but we forgot that God has his own plans. Oh Joe, my son."

"Get up, Mother, we must see to Emily. You've lost your youngest son and I my youngest brother. She's lost her husband and the father of her children. Get up, Mother."

Fons watched Jane. He had never seen anyone like her. He walked close to her and asked what he could do to help. She looked at him with an expression of surprise. "Where is the rider now? Thank you, Fons, for being here. Can you stay the night? Maybe you can sleep by the fire. We will comfort each other but your presence will be appreciated." She pulled her mother to her feet and they walked to Emily's side.

"The rider's gone to tell John Henry. They'll go on to Dock and Melissa. John Henry and Dock are the only sons of our family, Jane, and you and Melissa are the only daughters. Thank God Bill didn't live to see another son dead. Here, Jane. Take Carrie." She lifted the baby out of Emily's arms and into Jane's. "You have children to see to, Emily. Go with Jane now and start your grieving. In the morning you'll need to bring Mamie into your grief."

"I can go alone now, Mother Buchanan. I need to be alone. See to your mother, Jane. She needn't be strong for me." With that last comment she started for the room she and Joe had shared with their children.

Nancy turned her eyes around the room and slowly sank to her knees again. Maude took little Carrie while Jane sat on the floor holding her mother. She helped her to her feet and walked with her to her bed. Only then did Nancy let her tears flow and she and Jane cried together for son and brother.

◆

The grave stood ready for Joe Neal Buchanan's burial here on Buchanan's Ridge. His body had been prepared at the request of the railroad, and brought home in a fine wood casket by wagon. It now sat by the empty hole as the family and their friends stood by, waiting for the preacher to begin. I wonder if they were able to look on his handsome face for the last time?

The wind was still in this quiet place. Nancy and Bill's family and neighbors were buried here, starting in 1878. In Jane's time Elizabeth Hollifield Buchanan, and her sister, Sarah Hollifield, Lula, her father, William, then Texie Missouri, were here. Now Joe.

Jane, Nancy, and Emily stood beside their children and their families, three widows and children without a father. How often now, and in the past years, was this a common condition? What now? December 1908 would meld into 1909, and bring a different world for these three women.

We cannot know what was in their minds, only read the words that are left to lead us down the time in which they lived.

23

Little Switzerland, N.C., 1909

Louisa DeSaussure Duls published *The Story of Little Switzerland* in 1982. She wrote a well researched book about the group of Charlotte, N.C. men, led by Heriot Clarkson, who "discovered" the beautiful mountain on which they wished to build *"a few summer homes and possibly for a summer colony."* She gives her view of our relatives who inhabited this place. She also gives us a view of the behind-the-scenes events that moved the lives of Nancy Deweese Buchanan and her family.

Her book begins, *"It was June, 1909."* Yes, it was six months after Joe Buchanan's death and Emily was left a widow. Nancy Buchanan had inherited all the land, the house, and the implements and furnishings of the farm, where she and Bill had lived in Grassy Creek. At her death all of this was to go to Joe. It was arranged since Bill wanted Nancy and their daughter, Lula, to live in this house until their deaths and to be cared for by Joe. In June of 1909, Nancy was alive and would live until 1935. Joe was dead.

In the second sentence of the second paragraph of Ms. Dul's book, she wrote: *"Mr. Reid Queen and Mr. Floyd Gardner, real estate dealers in Marion, N. C. who, having been contacted by Mr. Clarkson* (Heriot Clarkson) *earlier, had arranged and led the expedition from Spruce Pine to Grassy Mountain, now began to point out by name the tallest peaks and deepest valleys visible from the flat top of this mountain nearly four thousand feet high: to the west, Mt. Mitchell, the Black Brothers, and Celo; to the south, Linville Mountain, Turkey Cove, the valley of the North Fork of the Catawba River, and, in the distance, the South Mountains; to the east and the northeast, Table Rock, Hawksbill, and Grandfather; and to the north, almost obscured by the brow of the mountain they were on and by the tops of chestnut trees, Roan."*

As Ms. Duls pointed out in her book, this crest was part of the Eastern Continental Divide. On page 2 of her book she writes, *"He (Mr. Clarkson) told Reid Queen and Floyd Gardner to look into the possibility of buying up land lying along the comparatively flat top of Chestnut Ridge* (known as Buchanan's Ridge and including the family cemetery) *and the lower slopes of Grassy Mountain. Then he hurried home to interest other business and professional men of Charlotte in his venture."*

On page 3, there is the written agreement between Reid Queen, Floyd Gardner, and Heriot Clarkson. Part of this agreement reads *"... that Reid Queen and Floyd Gardner have agreed with Heriot Clarkson as follows: That for Eleven ($11) Dollars an acre, and further sum of one dollar in hand paid, they will deed fee simple to Heriot Clarkson, ... all that land ... and to include what is known as the "Buchanan tracts," "Schism tract," "W. E. McCall tract," "Mrs. Catherine McNeely tract," "part of Hollifield tract," "T. M. McKenny {sic} tract," "D. M. Smith tract," "Robert and N. A. Hall piece," "G. R. Deal and piece of land Falls {Grassy Creek} are on."*

On page 5, paragraph two, of *The Story of Little Switzerland*, it states: *"In February, 1910, the (Switzerland) Company decided that one hundred acres of its land should be laid off in lots of one acre each and sold for not less than $150 per acre (the figure was moved up in 1913 to $300 and, by 1979, it was between $5,000 and $10,000 an acre)."*

◆

While searching Superior Court records at the Spruce Pine library for information on my grandfather, Fons McKinney, I came across the following:

Petition to Superior Court September 10, 1909 by Emily A. Buchanan, Guardian of Mamie Viola Buchanan and Carrie Josephine Buchanan, would respectfully show to the court that the said Mamie Viola and Carrie Josephine are infants under the age of 21 years. That the said infants are the owners as tenants in common of one half interest each in the tract of land in the County of Mitchell and State of North Carolina and in Grassy Creek Township, subject to a life estate of Nancy M. Buchanan.

The petition describes the land (100 acres) that she (Emily), as Guardian, has sold for the interests of the said infants, and the 55 acres and 4 acres, which Joe had inherited from his father, who had inherited it from his mother, Elizabeth Hollifield Buchanan. It was sold, for the sum of seven hundred and twenty five dollars, to Reid Queen, *"in the opinion of your petitioner, a fair price and the value of the said interests of the said minors. The petitioner has sold and conveys to the said Reid Queen her dower rights and said Reid Queen has purchased the life estate of*

Nancy M. Buchanan. " I saw no notation of any price paid to Nancy Buchanan for her life estate in this property, and as deeds show, she hadn't sold her dower rights. (I wonder if this fact would have made a difference to the Superior Court, allowing Emily to sell the 100 acres. We will never know the answer.)

No. 7 of the petition states: *"That the interests of the said infants will be materially promoted by the sale of their respective interest in said lands, so that the proceeds from the same may be invested by their (Guardian) in more desirable land for the benefit of said infants."*

I found the following records at the Register of Deeds in Bakersville, N. C.:

<u>Book 59, page 507</u>, July 13, 1909. *Option Contract for purchase of land between Emily A. Buchanan and Daniel L. (Dock) Buchanan to Reid Queen. General warrant of title free from all encumbrances except life interest of Nancy M. Buchanan, known as J. W. Buchanan (deceased) tracts, W. A. Buchanan house tract and part of H. M. (Molt) Schism (Melissa's husband) tract containing 100 acres, part acquired by inheritance from J. W. Buchanan, for $725. Paid $5. Balance to be paid when surveyed.*

<u>Book 57, page 579</u>, *October 5, 1909, Daniel L. (Dock) Buchanan and wife, Dovie, sold 41and 4/10 acres to Reid Queen for $414.00.*

<u>Book 60, page 83</u>, *October 7, 1909, Emily A. Buchanan sold to Reid Queen: 100 acres, subject to life estate of Nancy Buchanan, plus 4 acres, and 55 acres. Sold for $725, by order of Superior Court for Mamie Viola Buchanan and Carrie Josephine Buchanan*

It seems that Nancy Buchanan still has a life estate on 100 acres of land and according to history was able to use her house and estate until her death, although it was bought from Reid Queen by the newly named Switzerland Company. Part of this land and her house were sold some years after her death, I believe, to Manley Hollifield.

The Buchanan's now lived in Little Switzerland. Nancy had bargained that the Buchanan Cemetery would be kept in place and would always be there in perpetuity. There is still more information to come from a deed of trust that takes place in 1911. But in the meantime, life will go forward for this family.

24

Courage

The widows Buchanan (Nancy and Emily) and the widow Snipes (Jane Buchanan) continued to live in their home. The young children probably knew very little of the transactions made, or of the money that changed hands, although it's certain that The Switzerland Company caused some consternation in the community. I imagine that the Buchanan land sale was well known (but not the particulars, since some think that Nancy Buchanan is the one who sold her land to The Switzerland Company. They also thought Nancy's mother, Rachel, or her father, Charles McKinney, may have given Nancy this property.)

The men of the community were hired to build roads and would soon be called on for their fine rockwork and carpentry skills. This skilled work would be much in demand and was welcome employment. Fons McKinney, and his brothers, became known for these skills, so they would have seen better prospects for their future. (Fons built houses for the "summer people" during the coming years and his brothers, George Rufus, and Lafayette (Fate), were known for their rockwork.)

Fons began making it to church each Sunday. It wasn't easy for him or his family to come amongst the gossip about his divorce. The family and Fons had known these people all their lives, though, and most gave them support during these times. He made sure both he and Lawrence had their hair slicked back and wore nice enough clothes. He had decided that he and Jane Buchanan Snipes should marry, and went out of his way to make a good impression. He had also heard about Nancy approaching his uncle, G. R. Dale, about Jane renting the home where he grew up. Fons was the man Jane and Nancy had seen making the grounds ready. He was going to see that Jane lived in this house, but he intended to live there with her.

There were several problems he would need to overcome, as he saw it. First there was Nancy Buchanan, then Jane herself, and last, but not least, Effie. He hadn't missed the level stare Nancy gave him when he was giving his respects to them each Sunday. Jane was gracious, but Effie would glare at him and Lawrence. She wasted no time tugging on her mother's hand, trying to pull her away. He decided it was time to make another call on Jane.

(Another person who didn't welcome his marriage to Jane was his mother, Susie. Lawrence was back with Nora and Fons contributed money to his parents for his care. Susie didn't want to lose this income.)

◆

It was late spring and he waited until the afternoon, hoping to catch Jane outside tending her garden. He didn't want to compromise her reputation, since he now considered himself a suitor for her hand in marriage, instead of a family friend. Of course, this was another hurdle. She didn't know that yet. Should she be inside, he would ask her to take a walk and show him some chores that needed attending to. This might get them away from those in the house. His luck didn't hold. He found both Nancy and Jane preparing hills for potatoes. Nancy looked up as he approached.

He spoke before she could. "Mrs. Buchanan, I've noticed your barn needs some work. There're a few things you might need doing that I haven't noticed. I'm working on the road nearby. I could come by on my way home and do these chores."

Nancy spoke up. "That is right neighborly, Fons. Are you sure you can spare the time? You need to be teaching your son to do his chores in your spare time. I hear he's a handful."

"You're right about that. Maybe I'll bring him along. He's big enough that he is a pretty good hand." He looked at Jane, while she looked back and forth between her mother and him.

"Thank you for thinking of us, Fons. With no men folk on the place, we have to look to John Henry and Molt (Schism), and they have their own farms to work. I reckon you've heard that Dock is mighty poorly. Mother, I think it would help us out. Thank you, Fons. I hope you will let us pay you a decent wage for your time."

He shook his head, no. "It will be my pleasure to help out. I still remember when you were staying with your grandmother, Rachel, and I came by to help with the outside work. It was a satisfactory arrangement."

They all noticed Effie walking towards the house. As usual she glared at Fons, but didn't say anything. Nancy stepped up and gave her a hug. "Well, I hope you had a good day at school. Now you help your mother. Fons, will you walk with me. I can show you a few things that need fixing."

He looked at Jane and gave her a nod, tried to smile at Effie, but was sure it was probably a grimace, since his face was stiff with anger. Hopefully no one noticed.

◆

Nancy didn't waste any time. As soon as she and Fons were far enough away from Jane and Effie, she took his arm and pointed to a fallen log. It was well enough into the trees that they were out of sight. She walked to the log and sat down. Fons followed.

"Have you stated your intentions to Jane?" As he shook his head, Nancy nodded. "I didn't think so. Why do you think your suit will be welcomed? You're known in these parts as a hothead. I can look at your knuckles and see the scabs. Fighting is one way to settle things, but you might come out on the losing side. Look at Dock."

"You haven't mentioned my divorce. Some people think this is a blot on my soul and an unforgivable sin. I'm surprised I haven't been turned out of the church. Maybe that's still to come." Fons leaned forward starting to put his face in his hands, but stopped himself. He looked up at Nancy. "I had a good wife in Hattie Waycaster and she gave me two sons. One is living. I made a bad mistake in marrying Hester Stafford. I don't know the reasons she had for not wanting Lawrence and me. but she left us. Jane is a woman who I've known long enough to see who she is. If she would have me, I would try hard to be a good husband to her."

"How do you plan to support her, Fons? I'm sure you know that this land has been sold from under our feet. It's legal, according to the law, but I can only live here and tend this place until I die. I have some money put aside, but I'll be looking to my children to help take care of me in my old age."

"I expect you won't be the only one to come sniffing around," she continued. "Like Emily, Jane is considered a well-to-do widow. I'd like Jane to be able to choose, should she so desire, a husband who cares for her and not her property. What do you say for yourself?"

Fons looked at Nancy and didn't reply for a minute or two. "Mrs. Buchanan, you know my family. Pap and Mam have raised a big family. I won't get anything from them. So far I haven't accumulated much, but I'm still young enough, at 28 years, for good, hard work. It looks like The Switzerland Company is going to be hiring and paying decent wages. I believe I can make a living wage for my wife and family." With that exchange, Fons helped Nancy to her feet and they walked towards the outbuildings surrounding her home.

Fons stopped and turned to Nancy. "I've taken note of Jane for many years, Mrs. Buchanan. She loves and respects her family. I saw, first hand, how she cared for your mother, Rachel Lowery. She seemed to be a dutiful wife to Vance Snipes, and from all accounts stood up to the hardships she endured during his illness. I saw her grieving for her father, sister, and brothers. I consider Jane a prize, not for her wealth, but for her character and steadfastness."

Nancy turned her head and brushed tears from her eyes. When she looked at Fons, he was staring down at the ground. "That sounded heartfelt, Fons. Both you and Jane have been through hard times. Best keep your own council for a time. Time heals and you both may be able to make decisions better down the road some. Come and I'll show you some fencing that needs tended to."

Fons didn't want to wait. He wanted to know what Jane thought of him, both as a husband and a man. He knew he wasn't a prize to be sought after, even if it was just himself. With Lawrence as part of the bargain and Effie, Jane might rather go a round with a bear. Likely as not it might be like taking on a "painter" handling the two.

Maybe Nancy was right. Jane had been through a long ordeal tending Vance through his illness. He was still "tetchy" as a plucked goose after his time with Hester. Any excuse and he was raising his fists. Jane needed a strong shoulder to lean on, a calm man that she could depend on. Could he be that man?

◆

The next Sunday Meeting, Jane walked right up to him and Lawrence. Tugging Effie forward she spoke to him directly. "Effie and I would like you and Lawrence to come to dinner. You might as well know I've waited until Mother has gone to John Henry's for a spell, and Emily and the girls are visiting her family. You can't say this isn't a good time." Stopping for breath, she waited for Fons' reply.

"I expect we better go right on then, before folks start up talking. Come on Lawrence, no one will miss us at Pap's. Let's just walk on off, quiet like."

Effie was livid as she looked from her mother to Fons. "You didn't tell me we were having them to dinner." She looked around for an audience since she was going to pitch a fit, but she felt her mother's hand tighten on her arm. "Don't, Effie. We're going to walk home like normal folks. Come, Fons, Lawrence."

The four of them didn't say much on the walk home. The biscuits were baked and in the warmer. Jane lifted a heavy black lid to reveal browned chicken. She stirred the potatoes and moved them to be warmed. The smell of this succulent food brought Fons and Lawrence to their senses. "Where can we wash up, Jane? I wouldn't think of coming to your table without clean hands."

Effie sniffed. "You should have made sure that your hands were clean before going to church."

Jane shook her head. "I'll just pour a little hot water into the cold, there in the bowl on the table by the door. There's soap and a clean towel lying beside it. Just help yourself while I bring the food to the table. Effie, please pour milk in the glasses."

"Mama, this isn't right having a man here for dinner with us alone. What will people think?"

"Effie hush. Fons and Lawrence are our company. Now let us sit down and partake of this food. If you'll all bow your head, I'll say grace. *Lord, we thank you for our health, our families and friends, and this food. Amen.*"

◆

After dinner, complete with warm apple pie, Jane looked at Effie. "I want you to take Lawrence outside. You can sit on the porch or take him around and show him the farm. Fons and I will come and find you when I've cleaned the dishes. Do you understand me?"

Effie stared at her mother. Rising from her chair she turned to Lawrence. "Do you want to come?"

Lawrence smiled. "Do you have stock on this here farm. I'd like to see what kind of place you have. It don't look like much to me."

Effie's face turned an ugly red and her mouth opened, but one look at her mother and she closed it again. "Doesn't," she murmured. "It doesn't look like much." She walked to the door and looked back at Lawrence. "Are you coming or not?"

Fons took his arm and turned him so that he was looking into his face. "Son, I expect you to show good manners to Effie. She is a young lady and you remember how you are to act." With that advice, he released him, and watched as he walked through the door and Effie followed.

"I won't close the door, Mama, so if you need me, just call out." With that retort she walked across the porch and down the steps.

25

New Beginnings, 1910

"Now, Fons, you've been making some curious remarks to me, personal like. I think it's time you explained yourself." Jane looked directly at him and waited.

His heart started thumping like thunder. He felt he couldn't swallow. Well, you can do this so get to it, he thought. He did swallow but he was afraid it sounded more like a gulp. "Jane, I'm sure that I admire you. I have for a long time, with all due respect. I want you to know that I think highly of you and would like your permission to call on you as a suitor for your hand in marriage." He looked at her. She didn't reply for several minutes.

"Did you love Hester, Fons?" Jane's face had gone pale.

Fons broke eye contact. He turned back. "I want to be honest with you, Jane, and I would like you to return it to me." His face reddened but he didn't hesitate. "During the year or so after Hattie's death I was in a daze. I worked until I was so exhausted that I didn't have time to think about our life together, or mine and Lawrence's loss. When that time was up, I needed a wife, for myself and for Lawrence. Do you understand my meaning?"

"Did you love Hattie?" Jane asked.

Fons looked puzzled. "We were young and excited about being together. Our lives went forward with the usual hardships. I guess we were busy trying to be grownups; trying to learn to live up to them. Did you love Vance, Jane?"

Staring straight ahead Jane shook her head, no. "I didn't love him, Fons. Not when we married, nor when he died." Tears came to her eyes. "He was most respectful to me and I came to believe, loved me very much. I felt a failure that I was only able to feel respect for him, and pity. The pity I tried to hide for his sake but he knew I didn't love him. I will not live like that again."

"Do you want more children? You must have wondered if I am barren since Effie is the only child that Vance and I had."

Staring at the floor, he shook his head, no. "I don't believe you are barren, Jane. I think that Vance wasn't a husband to you after Effie's birth."

This was more than Jane could accept. Her face reddened with anger. "When I came to this house I made up my mind. I would make a life for Effie and me. I would not remarry." There was silence in the room.

Fons started to get up but settled back in his chair. "Would you consider what I asked you, let me call on you, knowing I want you for my wife?"

"Have you heard what I have expressed to you? Do you think you can learn to love me, as your wife?"

"I like you, Jane. I hold you in highest regard. These feelings for you are a good foundation on which to start a marriage. Can you tell me? Could you come to love me, as your husband?"

"I don't know what it would be like to know romantic love for a man. I only felt that I wanted, needed to feel something more for Vance. I knew, in my physical being, that he felt for me what I wanted to feel for him."

Fons was in new territory. "You didn't answer my question, Jane. I'm not talking of romantic love. Do you respect me as a man, could you honor me as your husband? This will be the basis on which love can grow."

Jane swallowed. Could she say what she knew in her heart? "Fons, I only know that I feel a pull towards you. I have for a long time. It is strong enough that I will agree to have you call on me as a suitor. I can't give you hope for the outcome."

◆

Jane Buchanan Snipes and James Alphonzo McKinney were married June 17, 1910. They had arranged to stay with Hettie and Jim Boyd that night. (Hettie McKinney Boyd was Uncle Tom and Aunt Jane (Dale) McKinney's daughter.) The plan was to keep Effie occupied, playing with the children, hoping she would fall asleep. They thought this would keep her from thinking about sleeping with her mother. "They" thought wrong.

Jane and Fons retired for the night before Effie knew what was happening. Either the door had a lock or Fons moved a heavy piece of furniture against the door. For sure, they had discussed this dilemma, and made plans accordingly.

When Effie realized they were gone she marched to the closed door and tried to open it. She lay on the floor and started kicking it. She kicked the door and cried most of the night. This is the story that has come down in family history.

Jane and Fons would have expected trouble. Lawrence was eight years old and Effie was eleven. Both of them were old enough to have plans of their own. The wonder is what happened behind those closed doors.

A woman like Jane would have her mind on her daughter outside the door. Effie made certain of that outcome. I would like to think that they spent time talking and making plans for the privacy they would need at home before falling asleep. In my mind, Fons would have held her in his arms as they slept. The other option would have her crying herself to sleep as he "laid down the law" about what would happen in the future.

We know from Effie that the time she and Lawrence spent under one roof was a volatile time for all concerned. It was a natural reaction under the circumstances, but I imagine a fair amount of discipline was needed, and dealt out. We also learned that Jane took the brunt of Lawrence and Effie's pranks. This and the fact that Susie, her mother-in-law, was not a friend, even holding a grudge against her, must have caused Jane undeserved pain. It seems that, for different reasons, both Susie and Nancy had been against this marriage.

26

Family

September 16, 1910, Daniel L. (Dock) Buchanan died. His three-year-old son, Carl, had also died that year. Dovie and their children mourned this terrible loss with Nancy and the Buchanan family. Dock had been in failing health since the knife fight, but had managed to care for his family before this final, fatal illness.

The family laid him to rest close by Elizabeth, Sarah, Lula, William, Texie, and Joe in the Buchanan Cemetery. (I don't know where William's father, Joseph H. Buchanan, is buried or Bill and Nancy's young sons, who died within days of each other in 1874. It's likely they are buried down in Turkey Cove.) Nancy now had two daughters and one son who would be with her at her death in1935.

Ida Jones McKinney was born to Jane and Fons McKinney April 22, 1911, in the two-story house down the slope from where Nancy Buchanan lived with Emily (Aunt Sis) Buchanan and her two daughters, Mamie and Carrie. The story is told that Jane served meals to nearby workers, and may have taken in boarders while living in this house. (Was she showing Fons that she could take care of herself?) According to Ida, (writing in her "Grandmother" book for her grandchildren,) "I was named for Mrs. Ida Clarkson Jones, who owned and operated Little Switzerland Inn, our first motel. Our family loved her." (My aunt, Mildred M. Whitener Coe, remembers Mrs. Jones asking Ida and sometimes, her sisters, to spend the night with her from time to time. She said it was lonesome before the guests started arriving.)

In August, 1911, a deed was made where Mrs. Nancy Buchanan and The Switzerland Company made the following exchange: *For value received, she was given a life estate in land in Mitchell Co. N.C., known as the H. M. Schism* (Melissa's former home place of 33 acres) *place in exchange for her life estate to all that piece of land known as the W. C. Summerville "lot" and all those lots fronting on the McCall Gap Road.* (I have no information about how or why this transaction was made.)

Jane sold the land she was to inherit from her father at her mother's death, to her brother, John Henry Buchanan, March 13, 1912, for $100.00. Nancy was, of course, still alive at the time. Thelma Anne McKinney was born to Jane and Fons, September 16, 1912.

In June of 1913, Fons bought 1.54 acres from The Switzerland Company for $125.00. He began building the house where he and Jane would raise their family.

Jane sold her former husband's estate, 60 acres in McDowell County, in October 1914, for $210.00. Effie was bitter about this sale for years. She thought she should have received this money. Jane gave her an acre of land at a later date, hoping to appease her. I don't think that it worked.

On January 2, 1915, Mildred Missouri McKinney was born in the new house. Effie married Fate McKinney, Fons' younger brother, in 1916. On February 17, 1917, Edith Rae McKinney (my mother) was born.

Mildred (Mickey) remembers their mother putting them in a big tub of warm water out by the spring one morning. She filled the wash pot with water after washing clothes. The pot would warm the water after the fire was out underneath. A black man walked down the road by their house, taking his weekly constitutional. He worked at the Switzerland Inn, so he wasn't a stranger to them. She remembers him laughing as the little girls peeked over the top, with just their eyes showing.

When Edith's eyes turned brown, Nancy made the remark that "a different bull must have been in the pasture for this one." (As my mother aged in her last years, she came to look like the pictures we have of Nancy except my mother's hair never turned white. My mother was a beauty, with deep dimples in her face, and had beautiful roan colored hair and dark brown eyes. I think Nancy may have been just as beautiful in her youth.)

27

A Gift

Nancy Buchanan had come for dinner again. It was a special occasion for her but she didn't let on. She felt it was time to make amends to her son-in-law. Fons, his brothers, and Lawrence, had worked hard for well over a year to get this house ready for their move from the house close by Nancy. They had other jobs and worked on the house in their spare time. That they were able to move in before Mildred Missouri (Mickey) was born was an accomplishment. Now Edith had been born here, too.

As they sat at the table for supper Nancy Buchanan spoke up. "Fons, I guess you saw I wasn't happy about your marriage to Jane. I thought with your past sorrows and Jane's, you both needed time. Now I see that you needed each other. With Effie and Fate married and Lawrence looking at going to the army, you've just got your young children here. Your past trials will always be with you, but now life is open before you."

The lamplight flickered around the dining table, lighting the faces of the four little girls, towheads all. Three had blue eyes and the smallest, in her mother's lap, had dark brown ones. They all looked expectantly at their dad while he looked at Jane. Mother Buchanan's sharp, dark eyes, peered from her little ruffled cap.

Fons looked at their daughters and then to his wife. Finally, facing his mother-in-law, he said, "I'm glad to have you at our table, Mrs. Buchanan. I apologize for going against your wishes, but Jane isn't someone on which I could wait. I'm happy that you see that we needed each other."

Jane smiled and lifted her head. "Fons, I won't speak for you, but we have seen how life and happiness come and then are gone. I've often wondered how people, like us, can just keep on picking themselves up after each blow. During my grief I've wondered how I could go on, yet I have. Mother has, and you, too. Now I have so much joy. What if I had let my early life take me down? This is my lesson. I wouldn't have missed our life. What we have here is a gift."

Nodding, he looked again at his family. He had Lawrence and Jane had Effie and now they had Ida, Thelma, Missouri, and Edith. "You are a brave woman, Jane, and I'm a lucky man to have you as my wife. I thank you." Looking down the dark hallway, he saw his children grown, grandchildren holding his hand, and Jane by his side.

◆

It's Christmas Eve, 1939. It was beginning to snow as the stars winked in and out. The little girl raised her arms to the sky, and tried to catch the cold flakes in her hands as she walked along. Her mother laughed, as the baby boy in her arms tossed around when the flakes touched his face. Dad gathered them up the steps, and raised his hand to knock on the door. It swung open, framing two beaming faces in the lamplight. A tall, slightly bent, white-haired woman gathered the little girl close, as her gray haired, blue-eyed husband ushered them all in by the fireside.

"I'm so happy to see you," she said. "Fons, take your grandson. He needs to see his grandfather." Browning eyes looked up at bright blue ones. Little hands reached for his nose and tugged. "Come, supper's ready. There's chicken and dumplings, apples and milk."

"Everything I like," says the little girl. She takes her dad's hand as she walks down the long, dark hallway to the dining room and kitchen. A lamp flickers on the table as she watches "Granny" and Mother bring steaming bowls from the kitchen. "Papa" pats his grandson as he sits down on the long bench at the table. "Uh, oh, Edith, you'd better see to your boy." She laughs as she takes him in her arms. "Yes, he just had his bottle as we came up the mountain. I'll bet he's ready to drop off, too."

As Granny fixes a cushion for her granddaughter beside Papa, Mother returned and took her seat. "I tucked him snug on the couch and he's fast asleep. We'll hear him if he wakes."

The little girl chimed in, "He cries pretty loud. Let's hurry up and eat." She looked out the dark window. "Santa's coming tonight, you know."

◆

The years go by and it's 1946. The fireplace lighted the darkening room and warmed us as we sat close by. We could hear the wind moan as it swept through the tall pines beside the house. That and the crackle and sizzle from the logs, accompanying the tick tock from the clock, made familiar music in this house.

Jane sat by the window fingering a pile of swatches as she chose another piece for her quilt. "Edith, do you remember this," she asked, holding a gingham piece up for her to see. "You wore this when you were just starting to school. It's a wonder, how long I keep these scraps."

Edith, sitting in a rocker, began giving Janice a bottle. The baby's blue eyes blinked up at her mother, a little fist curled around her finger. Edith looked at her mother, a smile beginning to deepen her dimples. "Mama, you've made a lot of quilts."

Jane nodded. "Yes, and with this cold weather you can't have too many. Maybe some day one of you will want this one." She bent her head and began stitching the swatch to a piece of blue serge. "Here's a piece from one of Fons' suits," she said.

Patsy leaned back against her mother's knee. "Can I help with the bottle, Mama?"

"She's finished I believe." She lifted the baby to her shoulder and began to pat her back. Edith looked down at her daughter. "You're old enough to help now, Patsy. Do you know how old the baby is? She will be one tomorrow."

A door opened and closed and footsteps came down the hall. "Here're the men folk," Jane said, as she put her quilting back in the basket and stood up. "It's only 4 o'clock but it's almost dark. Time to put supper on."

David walked in and took Janice, kissing Edith on the cheek. "We flushed a lot of rabbits, didn't we Daddy." Little Jim struggled out of his coat as he walked over to Patsy and put his cold hands on her face. Jane patted his arm as she started for the kitchen. "I love you, Granny," he said, looking after her. She stopped and turned to him. "I love you too, sweet one." Then she walked down the hall. "Come on, son, let's sit here by the fireplace." David sat down on the couch, holding Janice.

Fons was in the kitchen lighting a lamp when Jane came in. She filled a pot with water from the running spigot for the potatoes he had dug on his way in. He picked up a cabbage he had gotten from a box on the porch. He quartered it on the side of the sink, to be steamed after the potatoes cooked. "I think the pan of apples left from dinner and cornbread will do for supper," Jane said.

Fons pulled a chair close by the stove to poke the wood in the firebox. "Dave and I saw Fate at the store this morning. He and Effie have been so worried about their boys. They are looking for Lewis any day now, maybe Earl, too. The terrible war has been over a year now. I can hardly believe so many boys were killed or wounded." He got up then and put his arm around Jane. "Thank the Lord they're safe. And David, it's so good to see that family in there."

As he moved away, Jane began stirring eggs, baking soda, and buttermilk in the cornmeal. "Fons, can you go to the springhouse and get milk and butter for supper?

Take Jim, he'll want to help. Be careful going down the path, it's getting dark." He grinned as he walked out the door. 'Like a mother hen,' he thought.

After putting the cornbread on to bake, she began lighting lamps for the dining room and one to take to the living room. Fons came in and they stood for a moment looking into the half-light, then into another time. They watched their children running, laughing, down this hallway. Then it was quiet again, just the wind whistling past the door and murmurs from the living room.

Fons focused on his family sitting around the table. Nancy looked on as Jane smiled at him with a question in her eyes. "Fons, looks like you've been far away." He laughed. "Reckon I was daydreaming about what may be coming tomorrow, but today is where my eye will be."

Effa (Effie) Louisa Snipes, ca 1915.

Thelma McKinney holding Ruby McKinney (daughter of Effie and
Fate McKinney), Mildred (Mickey) and Edith McKinney.
Back row: Lawrence (son of Fons and Hattie Waycaster
McKinney), Fons, Ida and Jane McKinney, ca 1920's.

On pony Edith and Ruby McKinney. Front row, Lester McKinney, Thelma, Ida, Mickey, and Lewis McKinney. Back row, Jane, Fons, Effie and Fate McKinney. (Ruby and Lewis McKinney are their children). Fons, Lafayette (Fate), and Lester are brothers.

Friends for life: Elise Hakes and Edith McKinney, 1923.

Summer friends: On log, Mildred (Mickey) McKinney, Rosalie Avery,
Edith McKinney, DeBose Avery. Front, Isaac Avery.
Others unidentified. Ca 1920.

Harry Hand, sheriff of Orange County, Florida.

Summer Outing: Back row, Edith and Mildred McKinney, Harriet Hand,
Thelma McKinney. Front: Jane B. Snipes McKinney, Ida McKinney,
Buddy Hand, Dot, and Tobitha.

Ida Hand and Fons McKinney are the cooks on these outings.

Edith McKinney and Nancy Buchanan, ca 1930–31.

Harriet and Buddy Hand, with Ida McKinney, sitting on the bumper of
a touring car. Harriet and Ida are home for the holidays from
Lees McRae Institute.

Four Sisters. Back row, Edith McKinney. Front, from left: Thelma, Mildred, and Ida McKinney. Ca 1934.

Painting of "Three Sisters" by Frank Stanley Herring. Left to right: Thelma Anne McKinney, age 15, Ida Jones McKinney, age 17, Mildred Missouri (Mickey) McKinney, age 14. ca 1930.

Jane Buchanan Snipes McKinney, 1951.

Unfinished painting of Jane B. Snipes McKinney by her son-in-law,
Paul W. Whitener, "Mama Jane with her Bible." Gifted to
the author by the artist's wife.

Jane and Fons McKinney, ca 1940.

At home again. Front row, Jane B. Snipes McKinney, Thelma M. Sparks, Fons McKinney. Back row, Mildred M. Whitener, Effie S. McKinney, Edith M. Turner, and Ida M. Burleson.

Front row, Ida M. Burleson, Edith M. Turner. Back row, Gaylord Burleson and David Turner. 1939.

Papa, Fons McKinney, at work. 1951

"Papa's Barn"—Oil on canvas by Paul W. Whitener, ca 1939. Gift to the
author, by artist's wife.

Epilogue

In the years ahead the daughters and son knew Fons and Jane as good and caring parents. Fons' temperament was still "tetchy," but Jane stood as a calm center in any storm. According to Ida, Jane was the one to discipline. All Fons had to do was give one the "look" and they knew he meant business.

Effie and Lawrence had families who grew up close by and the nieces and nephews were like sisters and brothers to the McKinney sisters. Lawrence's children grew up loving and knowing Jane as their grandmother. Effie didn't care for her stepfather, but came to respect him as the years went by.

There are many pictures of the family together, and some of Ida, Thelma, Mickey, and Edith on outings with their friends, chaperoned by Fons and Jane. Harriet Hand, a summer friend, would become close to Ida and Thelma. My mother, Edith, grew up with Elise Hakes as a good friend and they stayed close all their lives. Her mother would become well known and part of this mountain community. (I remember going to Mrs. Hake's home with my parents to a "New England" boiled dinner as does my sister, Janice.)

Sometime in 1930, Jane and Fons' family met Frank Stanley Herring and his wife. He was an artist who was living in New York City and taught at the Grand Central Art Galleries School there. They stayed at the (Little) Switzerland Inn at first but later he and his wife rented a cottage within walking distance to the inn. Our family has a signed pencil drawing that he made of Nancy Buchanan in that year. He also had three of Fons and Jane's daughters sit for a painting. (Both are copied for this book.)

In *The Story of Little Switzerland* Louisa Duls tells of this painting, writing that four of the daughters sat for it. Although my Aunt Mildred (Mickey) told me that only three of them sat for the painting, she also said that none in the family had ever seen the finished portrait. My sister, Janice, and I were interested in finding the painting. We wanted to make sure that our mother (Edith) wasn't in the picture.

I met Everett Kivette when my husband and I moved to Burnsville, N.C. from Charlotte in 1996. Everett and his wife, Ruth, knew Mr. and Mrs. Herring, who founded the "Burnsville Painting Classes" (SeeCelo) with Edward Shorter, and ran this successful art school on a campus looking out toward Mt. Celo, from

1949 to 1965. (From 1947 to 1948 they conducted the "Burnsville Painting Classes" in what is known as "The Carriage House," while living at the NuWray Inn.) In 1966, after the death of Frank Herring, Everett, and John Bryans, who both studied with Mr. Herring and Mr. Shorter, founded "Painting in the Mountains" following in the tradition of the "Burnsville Painting Classes." Everett is now working to establish a Gallery and Archives to commemorate the life in art of the Herrings and others, for the new Yancey County Public Library that is to be housed in the historic old Yancey Collegiate Institute now being restored.

I told Everett about the missing painting. He was quite surprised that Mr. and Mrs. Herring had been in the mountains as early as 1930. He was also interested to know that Aunt Mickey had watercolors that he had painted of her when she was seventeen (1932), and a large portrait standing in her wedding gown (made by Jane, her mother), while it is being hemmed by Mrs. Herring and her cousin, both seated beneath her (1936). Aunt Mickey also has oil paintings: one a beautiful portrait of her that he painted about 1939, and a landscape that he gave to her and her husband as a wedding present. Mr. Herring was one of her husband's art teachers.

Everett found the painting of the "Three Sisters" at the Atlanta home of Mrs. Herring's niece, Mrs. Frank Stedman (Beth Hall). She brought it to Burnsville, where Mr. and Mrs. Kivette held a lovely dinner party for Aunt Mickey, to unveil the painting. It is life-size and portrays Aunt Mickey at age fourteen, Aunt Ida at age seventeen and Aunt Thelma, age fifteen. The photograph in this book is a copy of the one taken for the Burnsville N. C. newspaper, accompanying an article written by Everett Kivette. Mrs. Stedman has since given the painting to the Hickory Museum of Art, where Aunt Mickey presided as Executive Director for thirty-seven years. It is very sad that my mother wasn't included in the painting (she would have been twelve at the time) and that Aunt Thelma, Aunt Ida, and Mother, were deceased before the painting was found.

Jane, Effie, and Lawrence all had beautiful daughters and Effie and Lawrence had handsome sons. Fons kept a sharp eye on his daughter's beaus. He was known as an active member of the Republican Party and was suspicious of one of Mildred's (Mickey) boyfriends. He told her, "You know he may be married or he might even be a Democrat." My mother, Edith, being the youngest, sometimes felt left out of her sister's fun. Once she became old enough, the sisters double or triple dated. She was always proud that she was selected as Miss Spruce Pine (where she went to high school) when she was about sixteen years old. Her three sisters also took part in the contest. Aunt Mickey was first runner-up. Mother went to Greensboro and represented Spruce Pine in the Miss North Carolina contest.

Jane missed her daughters as they grew up and were taking part in activities that didn't include her or Fons. Nancy had been living with them and was loved as part of the family. Jane made notes in her Bible that she read through continuously, about how lonesome she was when her girls were out and she needed to stay home with Nancy. Jane also made notations in her Bible when her daughters were married. This was a time of all her happy memories, too.

"Down a dusty road, past the old apple orchard at McKinney's Gap, we went to Pepper's Creek," Jane told my mother. (I imagined the time, brown eyes lighting, as they turned to a time and place, a long, long, time ago.)

"Summer full trees crowd the winding road, water gurgles from a distant stream, and ferns wave as we go by. There's a road turning towards a weathered house, flowers by the door." (She visited here a long, long time ago.)

"Jane, come in. We're peeling apples on the back porch. Come through, it's cool out back. Have a cup of water right from the spring and rest your feet. Oh, it's so good to see you. How long can you stay?" (Were they cousins, aunts? Maybe Rachel, her grandmother was still there, then. Wouldn't you love to know these people who made our Grandmother Jane so happy? Love was here for her on Pepper's Creek, a long, long time ago.)

(I stand here near the trees and listen as the wind whispers her laughter, their happy voices. I see her sweet face and remember how much I loved to visit her a long, long time ago.)

Nancy Buchanan died August 26, 1935 in the McKinney home, a few months after my mother, Edith, was married but was still at home. Fons and Molt Schism (Melissa's husband) built her casket from walnut boards Nancy had prepared and kept for this purpose. They went to Spruce Pine and bought brass fittings and handles. The casket was sanded and polished and the family remembers that it was beautiful. She was buried beside her husband in Buchanan Cemetery. Judge Heriot Clarkson, my Grandfather Fons McKinney and Emily (Aunt Sis) Buchanan's second husband, George W. Butler, had a monument to Nancy placed in this cemetery. Knowing the story now, I can understand why these three men felt the need to honor her. Robert, Susan, and Nora McKinney, parents and sister of Fons, are also buried in the Buchanan Cemetery. They were neighbors in life and now in death.

My mother, Edith, married Dad on the sly and kept it a secret for several months while he got a home ready for her in Valdese, N.C. My dad, David E. Turner, grew to love Jane and Fons as his own family. He and my brother, Jim, hunted with Fons and other local friends. My mother, and Effie, were the daughters who learned to sew, quilt and crochet, keeping their mother's and grandmother's talents alive. Mother loved pretty clothes and made her own wardrobe. She and dad were talented and loving parents.

Ida, who studied to be a teacher, like her granddad, William Buchanan, married first. She and Harriet Hand (from Orlando, Florida) had gone to Lees McRae Institute (now Lees-McRae College) in Banner Elk N. C. together to finish high school. Harriet spent the holidays with the McKinney family. Ida and Harriet loved horses and were considered fine riders. (I remember going to a drugstore in Valdese with my mother when I was about seven or eight years old. She noticed a large postcard picture of a young woman sitting on a rearing horse. It was advertising Kodak firm. It was also a picture of my mother's sister, Ida. When Mother made that observation, the owner of the store hastily put it under the counter. Aunt Ida gave Mother a framed copy of this picture. After my mother died, we gave it to Ida's grandson, David McFalls.)

Ida studied with Mrs. A. E. Gouge in her last Teacher's Training Class. Later in life she attended East Tennessee State College and would get her B.S. from Appalachian University. She first taught in a one-room school in Little Switzerland. Her nieces, Ruby McKinney Buchanan and Betty McKinney Mace, were some of her first students. Later she taught many years in Spruce Pine, N.C. She and her husband, Gaylord Burleson, raised their family there.

A letter from Ida Hand, mother of Harriet and "Buddy" Hand, gives a window into the world of Jane and Fons McKinney.

Orlando, Fla. Nov. 29, 1928
Thanksgiving Day

My Dear Jane,

One year ago, today, Buddy and I, left your home for the South. I have thought of it often today and expect you have too.

Oh, how much we have to be thankful for—and one of the many blessings I am thankful for is you and your "Fons" and your people and your home.

May God bless your home and all its inmates and I trust some day it will be my pleasure to return to you the many favors you have always shown me and mine.

Well, my dear, I am wondering if Ida and Harriet were able to spend the day with you. I know they were anxious to go but know too that it is very cold and lots of snow so perhaps they did not.

Today is warm and balmy here, our doors and windows are wide open and we ladies are wearing our summer frocks.

How much I did want to go to Little Switzerland to see about things but after you wrote such a good letter saying Fons had looked after things I did not worry.

I am wondering though what has been done about the apples. Do hope he has been able to sell some. If there could be any saved, I think we would be tempted to take up a truck load of oranges and bring back a load of apples—but guess it is too late now. As no doubt the apples are all frozen.

Did you have a good crop of potatoes and how are they selling?

Mother was invited out today for turkey dinner. I am so glad that she can go. She is staying out here now.

You must feel quite "set up" with your two new rooms. I am sure glad that you have them and do trust there is a flue and that you had Fons go over and get the stove. It is such a nice stove and does not require much wood or coal.

Thursday night, one week later. Just read letter from Harriet, in which she says Baby Earl (McKinney) has been very sick with Scarlet Fever. Oh, how I hope the little fellow is out of danger. How dreadful that he should have Scarlet Fever. How did he contract it? Poor Effie (Snipes, McKinney), I know she must be worried and tired out too. Please let me know, if only a card, how he is.

Was glad the girls could go home for Thanksgiving, and do hope Harriet did not cause you any extra work. We are so anxious for her to come home Christmas but we are not sure yet. If she does not, and you can take her, I want to pay her board for you cannot afford to keep her for nothing. I just feel it is an imposition for her to always go to your house and I just can't let her unless I can pay her way.

I cannot send much "Christmas" this year but will send some little things to let the children know that I have not forgotten them. Must close now as I have much to do.

With love and best wishes.

Ida Hand

Effie, Fate, and their children led lives that were intertwined with Jane and Fons and Effie's four younger sisters. Effie and Fate were active in Chestnut Grove Church. Fate was a Deacon and leader of the choir. He was known for his fine rockwork, helping to build Chestnut Grove Church and other projects around the community. Effie was known as the Christian matriarch of Chestnut

Grove Community in her later years. She led many in pursuing their Christian vocations.

Ruby, their oldest daughter, although some years younger than my mother, was favored with Mother's teasing and remembers that she always came back for more. Lewis, the oldest, was born in the same year as Mother and she told me stories of their favorite antics. When he was just a young boy the family saw him riding a large hog. Asked what he was doing, he said, "Oh, just "widing awound."

One story that's often told is about Earl, the youngest son. He put his head in Effie's churn (to lick the leftover cream) and couldn't get it out. Effie was unable to get the churn past his ears. She picked up the churn and Earl and walked him down to Fons and Jane's house. Fons filed the metal straps holding the staves of the churn. As Earl was freed he said, "I knew Uncle "Fonie" could get me out." Betty, the youngest child, was my heroine. My favorite time was standing by to watch her make up her face and fix her blond hair.

Mildred Missouri (Mickey) married in 1936 and moved to Hickory, N. C. Her husband, Paul W. Whitener, became a well-known artist and founded the Hickory Museum of Art, the second art museum to be founded in N.C. Paul was the Executive Director until his death in 1959 and Mildred McKinney Whitener took his place on an interim basis but stayed on for thirty-seven successful years.

Early in their marriage, Mickey became the buyer for Charles of the Ritz makeup line at a department store in Hickory. She trained in New York City so she and Paul visited their artist friends there. They were very helpful by introducing them to artists and patrons who gifted and sold American Art to the Hickory Museum. One such friend was artist, Wilford A. Conrow, who lived in Carnegie Hall. The Conrows were close friends and Paul was his only student.

Thelma McKinney Sparks and her husband, Lawrence Sparks, were part owners of a laundry in Spruce Pine. I remember spending happy times with them as I grew up. Thelma lived close by Little Switzerland and she and Effie were the caretakers of the family. I remember a time when Thelma came to Valdese to get me so that I could help out when Granny Jane had a bad back. After her husband died in 1958, Aunt Thelma moved to Hickory, N. C. to live with Mickey, soon after Paul's death in 1959. She assisted Aunt Mickey in the museum for many years. (I have learned that Thelma was a wonderful dancer and was a popular partner at dances here in the mountains. It caused some consternation when young men came from out of town (Burnsville) to claim her as a partner. I remember a silver colored evening gown that she gave me to play in when I was about seven or eight years of age.)

These five sisters, Effie, Ida, Thelma, Mickey and Edith stayed close all their lives. I grew up regaled with stories of their growing up years and knew to expect that they would meet each year, the five of them, just to be together once more.

My mother and aunts said their father wasn't demonstrative of his feelings towards Jane as they grew up. The one time he kissed her in front of them was a shock. They said he had been working in Charlotte (for Heriot Clarkson) and when he came in the door he embraced and kissed her. They also said they were sure that their mother loved him and it was romantic love, too.

Many years later in his final illness, Fons held his daughters while talking of Jane. They remember him saying, "Girls, I want you to take care of your mother. She made a man out of me."

Fons had fallen ill with Hodgkin's disease when he was still a strong man of 68. He struggled with this disease until his death at age 72 on April 26, 1953. This was the same day that Jane's father, William Buchanan, died fifty years before. Jane was 77 at the time of her husband's death and had suffered ill health for some years.

The daughters didn't want Jane to stay in her home alone. She took turns staying with them and their families until her death at age 81 on August 28, 1956. Fons and Jane are buried at Burnette Cemetery, "among those stones on the hillside, above their church at Chestnut Grove." I know now of their courage and strength in their time. My eyes are drawn up to where they are *lifted to the shoulders of a mountain.*

Alphabetical List
of Characters by Surnames

Buchanan:

Alford A.

1. William A. Buchanan's brother. Killed at North Anna River, Virginia, May 26, 1864.

2. First son of William A. and Nancy Buchanan. Named for William's brother Alford A., called "Bud".

Daniel L. (Dock)—Fifth son. Married Dovie McBee.

Elizabeth (Hollifield)—William A. Buchanan's mother. Married Joseph H. Buchanan.

Freddie—Alford Anna Buchanan, daughter of Alford A. and Sallie Ann (Elliott). She married Salve McKinney.

(Mary) Jane—Second daughter of William A. and Nancy Buchanan. Married Zebulon Vance Snipes and second, James Alphonzo McKinney.

John Henry—Second son of William A. and Nancy Buchanan. Married Emma Jane Elliott, sister to Sallie Ann.

John Robert (Bob)—Brother to William A. Buchanan. Married Rebecca (Becky) Snipes, sister to Zebulon Vance Snipes.

Joseph H.—Father of William A. Buchanan. Married Elizabeth Hollifield.

Joseph (Joe) Neal—Sixth son of William A. and Nancy Buchanan. Married Emily A. Hollifield.

Lula E.—Third daughter of William A. and Nancy Buchanan. Invalid who died at age 21.

Maude—Daughter of Alford A. and Sallie Ann Buchanan. Lived with Nancy and William after her parents died.

Martha Melissa (Schism)—First daughter of William A. and Nancy Deweese Buchanan. Married Molt Schism.

Nancy (Deweese)—Daughter of Rachel Jane McKinney and Louis Deweese. Married William A. Buchanan.

William A. Buchanan—Son of Joseph H. and Elizabeth Hollifield Buchanan. He married Nancy Deweese.

Dale:

George Rufus—Father of Susan (Susie), Jane, George Rufus, Jr., and James Dale (others). He married Rachel Mace.

(George) Rufus, Jr.—Son of George Rufus and Rachel Mace Dale. Known as Uncle Ruf.

Jane (McKinney)—Daughter of George Rufus and Rachel Mace Dale. Married Tom McKinney, brother of Robert P. McKinney.

Rachel (Mace)—Mother of Rufus, Susan, Jane and James Dale (others). Married George Rufus Dale, second Mr. McBee.

Susan E. (McKinney)—Daughter of George Rufus and Rachel Mace Dale. Married Robert P. McKinney.

Deweese:

Jane (Washburn)—Daughter of Louis and Rachel M. Deweese. Married Daniel Mose Washburn.

Louis—Father of Nancy Deweese (Buchanan), Jane and Mary Elizabeth Deweese. Married Rachel Jane McKinney.

Mary Elizabeth (Biddix)—Daughter of Louis and Rachel M. Deweese. Married Francis Biddix..

Nancy Melissa (Buchanan)—Daughter of Louis and Rachel McKinney Deweese. Married William A. Buchanan.

Rachel Jane (McKinney)—Daughter of Charles and Elizabeth Lowery McKinney. Mother of Nancy, Jane and Mary Elizabeth Deweese. Married Louis
Deweese, second Alexander Lowery. Children: Elmira, Bakey, Aletha, Sam-
uel Alexander, Buenavista and John F. Lowery.

Elliott:

Emma Jane (Buchanan)—Married John Henry Buchanan. Sister to Sallie Ann
Elliott.

Sallie Ann (Buchanan)—Married Alford A. Buchanan. Parents of Alford Anna
(Freddie), and Maude Buchanan, others.

Hollifield:

Sarah H.—Sister of Elizabeth Hollifield Buchanan.

Lowery:

Alexander—Second husband of Rachel Jane McKinney Deweese.

Elizabeth (McKinney)—Legal wife of Charles McKinney. She was the mother
of Rachel Jane, and Alexander McKinney. The story that comes down in
the family has her dying shortly after her son, Alexander, is born.

McKinney:

Alexander—Son of Charles and Elizabeth Lowery McKinney. Brother of Rachel
Jane.

Charles—Father of Rachel McKinney Deweese Lowery and Alexander McKinney. Married Elizabeth Lowery. McKinney's Gap is named for him. Father
of Charles, Jr.

Charles, Jr.—Father of Robert Pendley McKinney, Thomas McKinney (and
others). Married Elizabeth Washburn.

Elizabeth (Lowery)—Mother of Rachel McKinney Deweese Lowery and Alexander McKinney. Married Charles McKinney of McKinney Gap.

George Rufus—Son of Robert Pendley and Susan E. Dale McKinney. Married Margaret Hollifield. Named for his uncle or great uncle, George Rufus Dale.

Hattie (Waycaster)—Married James Alphonzo McKinney. Mother of Lawrence and Wayne McKinney.

James Alphonzo (Fons)—Son of Robert Pendley and Susan Dale McKinney. Married Hattie Waycaster, second, Hester Stafford, third, Mary Jane Buchanan Snipes.

Jane (Buchanan, Snipes)—Daughter of Nancy Deweese and William A. Buchanan. Married Zebulon Vance Snipes and second, James Alphonzo McKinney.

Lafayette (Fate)—Son of Robert Pendley McKinney and Susan Dale McKinney. Married Effa (Effie) Louisa Snipes.

Lawrence—Son of James Alphonzo and Hattie Waycaster McKinney. Married Grace Collis.

Lester—Son of Robert Pendley and Susan Dale McKinney. Married Margaret Townsend.

Nora—Daughter of Robert Pendley and Susan Dale McKinney. Unmarried.

Robert Pendley—Son of Charles McKinney, Jr. and Elizabeth Washburn. Married Susan E. Dale.

Susan E. (Dale)—Daughter of George Rufus and Rachel Mace Dale. Married Robert Pendley McKinney.

Tom—Son of Charles McKinney, Jr. and Elizabeth Washburn. Married Jane Dale.

Wayne—Son of James Alphonzo McKinney and Hattie Waycaster. Brother to Lawrence McKinney. Died as an infant

Snipes:

Effa (Effie) Louisa (McKinney)—Daughter of Zebulon Vance Snipes and Jane Buchanan. Married Lafayette (Fate) McKinney.

Jane (Buchanan, McKinney)—Daughter of William A. and Nancy Buchanan. Married Zebulon Vance Snipes and second, James Alphonzo McKinney.

Rebecca (Buchanan)—Daughter of Patton and Margaret Curtis Snipes. Married John Robert (Bob) Buchanan, brother of William A. Buchanan.

Tom—Son of Patton and Margaret Curtis Snipes. Brother of Zebulon Vance and Rebecca Snipes, others.

Zebulon Vance Snipes—Son of Patton and Margaret Curtis Snipes. Married Jane Buchanan.

Stafford:

Hester—Married James Alphonzo McKinney. Divorced and remarried.

Waycaster:

Hattie—Married James Alphonzo McKinney. Mother of Lawrence and Wayne McKinney.

Land Deeds of James Alphonzo McKinney

According to deeds, Fons McKinney bought the following additional property from The Switzerland Company: March 1925, bought 1.20 acres for $100.00. June 1925, bought 1.70 acres for $170.00. September 1940 bought 1 acre for $100.00. Jane bought 1 acre from The Switzerland Company for $100.00 in September 1940. In June 1944, Fons bought 4.65 acres for $279.00. (We grew up hearing that our grandfather, Fons, and Judge Heriot Clarkson were good friends. Knowing that he was a Democrat and my grandfather was a staunch Republican lends interest to their relationship. This friendship could have accounted for the price he paid for land acquired from The Switzerland Company. I met Judge Clarkson's son, Attorney, Francis Clarkson, in Charlotte, N. C in the early 1970's. He remembered my grandfather with fondness.)

More letters of interest to the community of Little Switzerland in 1928:

NEW YORK
II WALL STREET

CHICAGO
209 SO. LA SALLE STREET

INDIANAPOLIS
41 N. PENNSYLVANIA STREET

THOMSON & McKINNON
BROKERS

MEMBERS
NEW YORK STOCK EXCHANGE
NEW YORK COTTON EXCHANGE
NEW YORK PRODUCE EXCHANGE
NEW YORK COFFEE & SUGAR EXCHANGE
CHICAGO BOARD OF TRADE
CHICAGO STOCK EXCHANGE
WINNIPEG GRAIN EXCHANGE

66 EAST CENTRAL AVENUE
ORLANDO, FLORIDA

FLORIDA OFFICES
JACKSONVILLE
ORLANDO
TAMPA
ST. PETERSBURG
PALM BEACH
MIAMI

Nov 1/28

Dear Jones/ The time is drawing near when we will all have an opportunity to vote for Herbert Hoover. It looks very much like Hoover will carry Florida and from what I read he will also carry Nor. Carolina. I am anxious to learn the result from your voting precinct and would appreciate it very much if you will mail me the result. We are having beautiful weather here but need some rain. With kindest regards to yourself and family I am

Your friend
W. E. Nivin

147

Preston & Ross
ATTORNEYS & COUNSELLORS AT LAW
Charlotte, North Carolina

200-205 LAW BUILDING

E. R. PRESTON
R. MARION ROSS

May 14, 1928.

Mr. Fons McKinney,
Little Switzerland, N. C.

Dear Sir:

As Judge Clarkson probably told you, one of
my boys was taken ill just as I started to Switzerland.
I have told Mrs. Jones so many tales about when I was
coming that I don't expect to write her any more,
but merely drive up. It is my hope to do so on Saturday
the 19th.

In the meanwhile I will stand by Judge Clarkson's
directions to you to go ahead. I had set $1500 as the
maximum to put in the house, and if by using cheaper
material or in any other way you can cut the price to
that figure, please do so. If not, let me know how
much reduction you can make and about when we can expect
possession and what sort of payments you will want as
we go along. Mr. Francis Clarkson said he would arrange
a loan for part of the purchase money so that you can
get all of your money upon satisfactory completion of
the house.

Please write me, so that I can have a regular
written contract, with plans attached agreeable to you
and Mrs. Preston, drawn up in typewritten form and bring
it with me when I come. In the meantime, please don't
lose any time.

Yours very truly,

E. R. Preston

ERP:L

P.S. Please let me know what arrangements can be
made about putting bark on the house, and the approximate
cost.

cc: Judge Clarkson

*Since dictating writing above Mrs Jones has
telephoned you will deduct $175 making $1525*

978-0-595-43750-4
0-595-43750-8

CPSIA information can be obtained at www.ICGtesting.com
Printed in the USA
BVOW032143070713

325228BV00001B/3/A